THE
BIG BOOK OF
GROSS
STUFF

THE
BIG BOOK OF
GROSS
STUFF

BART KING
Illustrations by Russell Miller

GIBBS SMITH
TO ENRICH AND INSPIRE HUMANKIND
Salt Lake City | Charleston | Santa Fe | Santa Barbara

First Edition
14 13 12 11 10   5 4 3

Text © 2010 Bart King

Illustrations © 2010 Russell Miller

Published by
Gibbs Smith
P.O. Box 667
Layton, Utah 84041
1.800.835.4993 orders
www.gibbs-smith.com

Designed by Michel Vrana
Manufactured in Shenzhen, China in January 2010
by Toppan Printing

Gibbs Smith books are printed on either recycled, 100% post-
consumer waste, FSC-certified papers or on paper produced from
a 100% certified sustainable forest/controlled wood source.

Library of Congress Cataloging-in-Publication Data

King, Bart, 1962-
The big book of gross stuff / Bart King ;
illustrations by Russell Miller. — 1st ed.
p. cm.
Includes bibliographical references.
ISBN-13: 978-1-4236-0746-5
ISBN-10: 1-4236-0746-5
1. Curiosities and wonders—Humor. 2. Human body—
Miscellanea—Humor. 3. Hygiene—Humor. 4. Conduct of life—
Miscellanea—Humor. I. Miller, Russell. II. Title.
PN6231.C85K56 2010
818'.607—dc22

2009035220

THIS BOOK IS DEDICATED TO YOUR DIGESTIVE MUCUS.
(AFTER ALL, NO ONE EVER GIVES IT A PROPER
"THANK-YOU"!)

CONTENTS

A NOTE ON THE WRITING OF THIS BOOK

This book really IS about gross stuff. And that's a tricky subject! Because when it comes to grossness, there is an invisible line between "hilariously funny" and "going too far." And just to make things interesting, that invisible line is different from person to person.

This means that this book is almost guaranteed to make you laugh *and* to actually gross you out. But, hey, don't chicken out now! After all, I had to be brave just to write all this stuff. You see, as this book's author, I face a unique danger. People might link ME with the disgusting things I'm writing about!

Not wanting to be contaminated in this way, I've taken special steps to ensure that I myself am *in no way gross*. So during the writing of this book, I stopped manufacturing:

★ mucus
★ dandruff
★ tweets from my Twitter

Furthermore, I showered twice daily. This process included exfoliation, defoliation, and deforestation. (Plus, I scrubbed between my toes!)

Finally, before sitting down to write, I looked at pictures of kittens, flowers, and puppies. This helped purify and protect my mind from the horrible topics that my cruel editor forced me to research.

As you can see, I have sacrificed a lot for this book, but as long as you do not associate me with grossness, it will have been worth it. And please don't link the following people with gross stuff either, even though they did help with this book: Lynn King, Matt Grow, MD, Parker Swanson, Virginia and Dallas Wassink, Michael Milone, the Groh family, Jeff Holiman, Chuck Shepherd, Carolyn Wood, Nancy Tipton, MD, Taewon and Philip Laplante, Jennifer C. Felton, MD, Robert Rowzee, Andrew R. Brown, MD, Michelle Herrmann, Robert Wilkes, Mary McLean, Annemarie Plaizier, Destiny Covington-Zawasky, Jennifer Blair, Kathleen Twomey, Tama Filipas, Dean Hanson, Lorraine Roosevelt, Don Sisler, Katy Killilea, Robin Henderson Thomas, Katie Greenseth, Dee Roosevelt, Christine Mathews, Tiffany Denman, Dave Sohigian, Debbie Alvarez, Jared Smith, Madge Baird, and Suzanne Taylor.

Well, as you're about to find out, it's a gross, gross world out there. Let's learn all about it!

WHAT MAKES IT GROSS?

"Dude, that's gross."

I bet you have heard someone say this recently. No? Then read this! A man from Belgium named Wim Delvoye made a machine out of thirty-three feet of laboratory tubes, along with various containers and gauges. The machine has a hole at both ends. To activate it, a cook "feeds" a meal into one end, and the big machine starts grinding up the food and moving it along.

Spectators then watch as the food makes stops at six vats of acids and enzymes. Finally, it works its way to the end of the process, where it comes out in a brown log.

And that's when everyone starts taking lots of photos.

Yep, it's a mechanical digestive system! But can you explain to me why people would stare in fascination at a machine that does the EXACT SAME THING that they can do?

BECAUSE IT'S GROSS!

No one ever says so, but gross stuff is sort of magical. Nasty things are like magnets that repel and attract us at the same time. Once our disgust is activated, we get a strong feeling of revulsion; we might start breathing through our mouth or look away from the gross thing in question. But at the same time, we can't help sneaking a glance (or a sniff) to see if that nasty thing is still oozing, stinking, or pulsating. (Yeah, pulsating is good!)

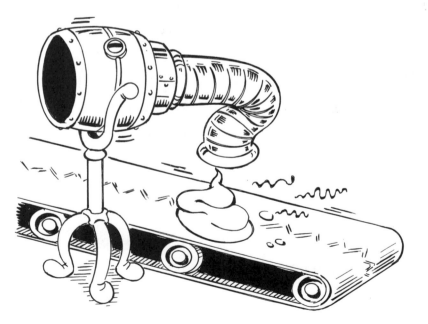

SPOT THE PATTERN!

Did you know that "nastify" (to make nasty) is an actual word? Neither did I! See if you can spot what all these words have in common! (Besides being gross, I mean.)

CLAMMY	ICKY	SLIMY
DANK	MOIST	SLIPPERY
FILMY	MUCILAGINOUS	SQUISHY
GLOPPY	MUCKY	STICKY
GOOEY	OOZY	TACKY
GREASY	SCUMMY	VISCOUS
GUMMY		

Do you see it? One way or another, all of these words are wet, or at least damp. And there are a lot of them. The only dry gross words I can think of are *scabby* and a few words that mean "filthy" (e.g., dirty, grimy, grubby). Then there are general-purpose gross words like *vile*, *noxious*, and *abhorrent*. But other than that, gross means *wet!*

Still don't believe it? A Web site called Visual Thesaurus asked its readers to rate how much they like or dislike certain words. And the second-most-hated word was "moist." (A friend once said that she dislikes cake mixes that are advertised as being "extra-moist" because that basically means "super-dank"!) Oh, and the most-hated word of all was "hate." So a lot of people hate hate.[1]

1.   Other hated words included *vomit, ointment,* and *slacks*. As one smarty-pants said, "I hate that my slacks are moist from where I vomited ointment on them."

13

Part of the appeal is that anything really gross is thought of as "off-limits." And anything off-limits is immediately tantalizing. So it works like this: "Don't look! *Hey, I told you not to look!*"

Isn't that weird? No other animal is fascinated by gross stuff, because no other animal ever gets disgusted! If, for example, a dog wants to avoid something putrid, it just steps to the side and continues on with its life. What it *won't* do is start jumping around and shouting, "Oh, my, that dead squirrel is loathsome!"

So apparently only humans feel the emotion of disgust. And it really is an *emotion*, just like love or hate, or like that feeling you get when a person has a piece of toilet paper stuck to the bottom of his shoe and everyone is laughing, but the guy is totally clueless—what's that emotion called? Oh yeah: relief that it's not you.

Now, think about how powerfully your emotions can affect you. If you're really happy, you laugh. If you're really sad (did someone give you this book as a gift?), you cry.

WORDS THAT SOUND GROSS (BUT AREN'T!)

AMBISINISTROUS: Clumsy; the opposite of ambidextrous.

ANONYMUNCULE: A generic little person.

BIFURCATE: To separate something into two parts.

COCCYX: A tailbone. You have one.

CORPUSCLE: A small cell, usually a blood cell.

DEBAG: To remove someone's pants as a "joke."[2]

EUMORPHOUS: Well formed, as in, "Dad, this meat loaf is eumorphous."

FARD: To cover one's face with makeup.

FINAGLE: To get something by cheating.

FLANGE: A thing that sticks out of something. (Yes, that is the worst definition of flange ever given.)

FUNGIBLE: Something that can be replaced.

GOBEMOUCHE: A person who believes anything.

GOULASH: A Hungarian stew.

---

2.   " 'We ought to debag him,' he cried. Appleby was thereupon debagged; but as ... he continued to walk about trouserless and dispense hospitality without any apparent loss of dignity, the debagging had to be written down a failure." Edward Compton Mackenzie, *Sinister Street.*

GRINAGOG: A person who smiles a lot.

JENTACULAR: Having to do with breakfast.

KANKEDORT: An awkward situation.

MAMMOTHREPT: A spoiled kid.

OSCULATE: To kiss, as in, "Timmy osculated his grandmother!"

QUAG: To shake something soft and flabby. (Hmmm, that actually *is* sort of gross …)

QUISQUILIOUS: Relating to garbage. (Hey, this one is gross too!)

SCROD: A young cod or similar fish. (Now *that's* more like it.)

SEQUACIOUS: Likely to follow the opinions and instructions of other people.

SEEPAGE: Stuff that is seeping. This word can be used with almost any gross word to brutal effect, i.e., butt seepage, booger seepage, cheese seepage, underwear seepage, etc.

SHIITAKE: An Asian mushroom.

"STOP QUAGGING ME!"

SPITCHCOCK: A way of preparing eel for a meal.

STORGE: Instinctive affection, like the kind you have for this book.

TARDILOQUENT: Speaking slowly.

TURGID: Puffed out.

UMBRIPHOLOUS: Fond of shade.

ZUGZWANG: Having to make a move in a chess game, despite the fact that there are no good moves available.

But if you're really disgusted, you barf. Beat that! Clearly, disgust is the most powerful emotion of all. But perhaps because of its vast power, some people think that disgust is just a feeling. These people have confused the emotion of disgust with the feeling of nausea. Fools!

BUT WHAT IS IT THAT MAKES SOMETHING DISGUSTING? FAMED SCIENTIST CHARLES DARWIN PONDERED THIS QUESTION IN 1872.

His theory was that disgust is universal to all cultures. And he was right! Let me add to this my belief that there is a sliding scale

17

of disgust that starts with the distasteful (e.g., bad breath) and goes to the revoltingly nasty (zombie breath). Some examples on the scale from least gross to most gross:

DISTASTEFUL (SLIGHTLY OFFENSIVE)

- ★ A burp
- ★ A dry booger
- ★ A sweaty T-shirt
- ★ Discovering you have acne
- ★ Thinking you might be able to smell someone's swamp gas

DISGUSTING (OFFENSIVE)

- ★ Someone who burps loudly, then says, "I can taste my lunch!"
- ★ A slimy booger
- ★ A sweaty T-shirt with a bloodstain
- ★ Popping a zit and having the pus hit the mirror
- ★ Poop

REVOLTINGLY DISGUSTING (SO OFFENSIVE, YOU DON'T EVEN WANT TO THINK ABOUT IT)

- ★ Someone who burps loudly, says, "Oops!" and then vomits
- ★ Seeing someone else pop a zit while they cut one at the same time
- ★ A T-shirt drenched in sweat, blood, and pus. (And it's yours!)

★ Oozing, slimy poop on a finger. (And it's yours!)

★ A putrefying, slimy dead body that stinks. (And it's—
wait, that wouldn't make any sense!)

C an we define WHY some things are grosser than others? Maybe! It seems like the most disgusting things either have to do with death and/or body fluids and discharges. And something really nasty often has the potential to "contaminate" you. In other words, just by being close to a slimy booger (germs!) or a dead body (zombie germs!), you might get infected and contaminated in some way.

The actual feeling of disgust comes from two places. One part of disgust is in your mind. Let me give an example. In a grossness experiment, volunteers were given identical vials. These vials had been prepared to contain a "decaying" odor. One group of the volunteers was told the vials contained cheese. And many of them reported *liking* the smell.

POP QUIZ!

Who do you think is easier to gross out:

Young people or old folks?

Women or men?

A study done in 2002 by the London School of Hygiene showed that young people are easier to gross out. (So much for prissy old-timers!) Also, *women are easier to gross out than men*. (What a stunner!)

19

POP QUIZ!

There is only one bodily fluid or discharge that is not rated as disgusting by the majority of people. What is it?

Eye juice, or what you humans call "tears."

But the other group was told that their vials contained poop. These volunteers freaked out! Oh, the smell was so horribly disgusting, they just couldn't stand it. Vile vials! Get them away! (Of course, the only difference between the vials was in the smellers' minds.)

This brings me to the second part of where disgust comes from. It's believed that recognizing something as gross is actually an instinct. At least, that's what Dr. Valerie Curtis says. And she studies diarrheal diseases (diseases involving diarrhea!), so I guess she would know. Dr. Curtis believes that disgust has helped keep humans from going extinct.

Curtis's studies suggest that almost every culture finds things having to do with poop, puke, spit, blood, sweat, and pus disgusting. Why? Since every human has a biological reason to avoid disease, we just might have a "disgust" gene in our DNA that keeps us alive. And that's why you naturally avoid poop (*right?*): so that you can steer clear of its disease-causing viruses and bacteria.

What happens if your body gets contaminated by one of these awful things? It kicks into overdrive disgust mode.

MAGICAL SPIT-SWALLOWING ACTIVITY!

To illustrate the strange ways that people view grossness, do the following:

First, get a volunteer. (Sure, you could do this yourself, but why would you? This activity is gross!)

Second, remind the volunteer that he or she has been swallowing his or her saliva all of his or her life. (Whew! That took a while to spit out!) Your volunteer will nod in understanding.

Third, hand your volunteer a glass. Tell the subject to spit repeatedly into the glass for five minutes.

Fourth, after the five minutes are up, check and see how much saliva is in the glass. There might be quite a bit! Now command your volunteer to drink it.

Carefully note your volunteer's reaction. The subject will probably exhibit disgust and refuse to drink the spit. Remind the volunteer that there was nothing disgusting about their spit up to this point. Even so, it is unlikely that this spit will be drunken. Dranken? Consumed!

Conclusion: This experiment shows the magical nature of disgusting things. By simply spitting spit into a glass, it becomes unswallowable. A magical transformation comes over it, and the normally innocent saliva becomes gross spittle!

MONEY IS THE ROOT OF ALL GROSSNESS

Not everything that's disgusting involves slimy stuff. Take money, for example. It's usually pretty dry! But every coin and bill you handle has been handled before you touched it ... and that means most money is swarming with bacteria, viruses, and spores!

A study of one-dollar bills being used at a high-school snack stand found that 92 percent of the bills had some germs on them. And 7 percent of the bills had harmful bacteria (like *Staphylococcus aureus* and *Klebsiella pneumoniae*) that can cause serious illness!

Moral: Wash your hands after handling money.

And you may not even be aware of it until you start throwing up. That's because there is something inside you called the "gut brain." This is a network of nerve cells that run in and out of your whole digestive system. If your gut brain detects food poisoning that's coming from a rancid piece of pork inside you, it will try to eject that putrid pork as quickly as possible: BLEAUGH!

But disgust is not just a response to danger. If it were, we'd be grossed out by mean pit bulls and poisonous mushrooms. But the fact is that you might not have much of a problem walking by a house that has a barking pit bull behind a high fence. And if you met a friendly pit bull, you might pet it, even though it could theoretically bite your face off. But if you saw a giant ugly black rat behind a neighbor's fence, you would cross the street to get away. Why? *It's a rat!* Even if its owner told you that the rat was friendly and germ-free, you would probably still avoid it, because disgusting things are STILL disgusting even when they're not dangerous! (So I'm guessing you wouldn't pet the black rat either.)

Here's another example. To almost all people, a corpse is really gross. But a lot depends on what *species* the dead body is! The closer the body is to a human, the grosser it is. Most people aren't freaked out by seeing a freshly caught dead trout, but if they see a dead chimpanzee, yikes!

But whether it's logical or not, disgust can help to educate us. For example, there are places in Pakistan, India, and Bangladesh where people have been pooping out in the open for centuries. And because of this tradition, the people

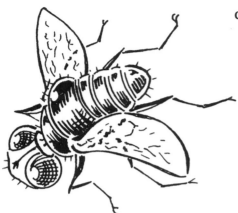

can see no reason to change their ways, even after new indoor bathrooms are built!

And so sanitation experts have learned this effective technique: they present an outdoor feast for the people of a village. This feast takes place near the spot where the people poop. While the villagers gather to eat and talk, the sanitation experts quietly scoop up some of the human poop that's nearby onto a plate. Then they set this plate near the food. Soon, flies come to land on the poop. Then the flies land on the food. No speech could ever make the reality of gross contamination more obvious!

And the next time the experts visit the village, the odds are that the people will be healthier because they're using their new indoor bathrooms.

THANKS, GROSS STUFF!

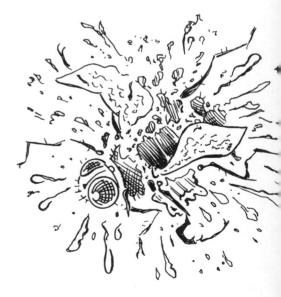

GROSS QUIZ!

Before you read any further, you might want to take this important quiz to learn how your views compare to the rest of society.

I. WHAT'S THE PROPER AGE TO STOP FARTING IN PUBLIC?

a. 9

b. 19

c. I will be farting at my own funeral.

2. YOU GO TO SOMEONE'S HOUSE FOR DINNER AND FIND THAT THEY HAVE MADE BABY RABBIT STEW AND LAMPREY SURPRISE. ("SURPRISE! WE MADE LAMPREYS!") YOU . . .

   a. Flee the house screaming.

   b. Eat a little bit of the food while smiling politely.

   c. Ask, "Could I have more baby rabbits, please?"

3. WHICH OF THE FOLLOWING BEST DESCRIBES YOUR MATURITY LEVEL?

   a. You've always gotten along better with adults than kids.

   b. You're as mature as most people your age.

   c. *Hee hee!* "Mature" rhymes with "manure"!

4. EEP! SOMEBODY CUT A BAD ONE. YOU . . .

   a. Organize a protest march.

   b. Breathe through your mouth.

   c. Compliment the offender.

5. DRIVING ALONG, YOU SEE SOME ROADKILL, PERHAPS AN UNLUCKY ARMADILLO OR LUWAK (SEE P. 236). YOU . . .

   a. Turn up the radio and accelerate.

   b. Shake your head sadly at the fate of all living things.

   c. Pull over and start searching your car for a spork.

6. THE PHONE RINGS. YOU ARE ON THE TOILET. DO YOU ANSWER IT?

a. No!

b. Only if you are expecting a call.

c. Yes, and you supply the caller with a play-by-play account of what's happening.

7. YOU OVERHEAR A CUSTOMER AT A CLOTHING STORE ASK FOR SOME PANTS WITH "MAXIMUM ABSORPTION."

a. You quickly distract yourself to avoid thinking about the situation.

b. You wonder: Which absorbs more fluid, cotton or wool?

c. You introduce yourself to the customer and show off how much fluid your trousers have already retained.

8. IF THE ALTERNATIVE WERE STARVING TO DEATH, YOU WOULD DECIDE TO EAT ...

a. Haggis (see p. 253).

b. Your worst enemy's poop.

c. A person.

9. A FRIEND OF YOURS HAS SOMETHING HANGING FROM HER NOSE, PROBABLY A BOOGER. SHE DOESN'T REALIZE IT. YOU ...

a. Concentrate on looking at her forehead and mentally go to your "happy place."

b. Make eye contact and then meaningfully point to your nose and make a swipe at it.

c. Lean in and say, "You have lovely mucus."

10. IF YOUR BROTHER SAYS THE WORD "SPUTUM," YOU WONDER . . .

a. Where your passport is, and how quickly you can book a flight to Italy.

b. How he got such a big vocabulary.

c. Whether he actually means mucus, snot, or phlegm (see p. 217).

For each question you answered with the letter "a," give yourself one point. For each question you answered with the letter "b," give yourself two points. For each question you answered with the letter "c," give yourself three points.

IF YOU SCORED FROM 10 TO 14, YOU MAY BE ONE OF THE FOLLOWING:

THE ACCOUNTANT: "Dude, that's the third time you've farted today." Although the accountant does not tolerate gross stuff, he does a really good job of keeping track of it!

THE PRISSY OVER-REACTOR: "I've never smelled anything so horrible in my LIFE!" Does this sound familiar? It should, because when it comes to making a big deal about gross stuff, this is you.

THE FAKER: Are you really that squeamish? (Or is it possible that, while you *say* you can't stand gross stuff, you secretly *love it?*)

IF YOU SCORED FROM 14 TO 26, YOU MAY BE:

THE PHILOSOPHER: You have a matter-of-fact way of looking at the world. Your relaxed attitude gives you good perspective, and so you are unlikely to get too worked up over gross stuff.

IF YOU SCORED FROM 27 TO 30, YOU MAY BE:

THE ENTHUSIAST: You're so enthusiastic about gross stuff, you always do everything bigger, stinkier, and with more mucus than your friends do. You may sometimes be viewed as a little creepy (and even subhuman!) by "normal" people. This is horribly unfair, except in cases where you actually ARE creepy and subhuman!

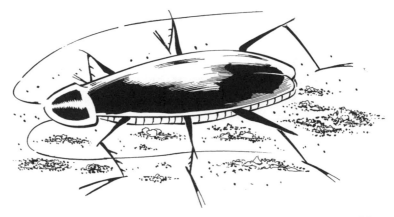

The Miracle of Birth

Trying to explain the facts of life to kids can be very tricky. So to get out of this, some adults just skip the whole thing. ("We found you in a pumpkin patch.") More common are adults who only tell part of the story. For example, read this story about a five-year-old I'll call "Timmy." Timmy had just started kindergarten when his parents told him to expect a baby brother or sister sometime in the future.

So at show-and-tell the next day, Timmy told his class the good news!

A month later, Timmy's mother was really beginning to show her pregnancy. She let Timmy put his hand on her stomach and feel the unborn baby moving inside her! After putting his hand on his mom's belly, Timmy gave her a funny look.

The next day at school, Timmy's teacher asked, "What's new with that baby your family is expecting?"

Timmy looked around and whispered, "I think my mom *ate* it."

Oh no! Luckily, Timmy's teacher explained to him that his mother hadn't really eaten the baby. Good for her! Then she went on to say that there is probably nothing more wonderful and life affirming than seeing a baby being born. Yes, she told Timmy that witnessing a new person's entry into the world is amazing. You get to see the first breath that person will ever take. And as a special bonus, babies are really cute!

Lies, lies, LIES.

My research has revealed that the birth of a baby is one of the most disgusting things ever! Thank goodness you have no memories of this horrible

PICK YOUR POISON!

Until recently, women who couldn't have babies didn't have babies. But in 1966, doctors came up with a new fertility drug. The only way to make it, though, was to collect the urine of elderly women or to harvest pituitary glands from dead women.

nightmare.[1] I mean, come on! First, the build-up for the big day takes months. (Nine of them, in fact.) And during this time, the pregnant mother blows chunks over and over again. This is because the hormones in her body throw her whole system out of whack. But it may also be nature's way of preparing the mother for the grossness yet to come!

Okay, sure, I'm exaggerating a little. Birth really ıs a beautiful, wonderful miracle. But everyone already knows that. So to even it out a little, I'm here to concentrate on the gross stuff—

EATING POOP FOR THE GREATER GOOD

Just like humans, animals often "poop their pants" when giving birth. (Yes, yes, I know that most animals don't wear pants.) And some of these animal mothers will then EAT the poop! Disgusting, you say? Maybe. Some people think this is a way for the animal to remove evidence of the birth so that enemies and predators won't steal the newborns away. It's also likely that mothers eat their own feces to keep vermin and insects away from their babies. (Or maybe it just tastes good!)

1. If you *do* have memories of this horrible nightmare, please ignore that statement.

IF YOU LOVE SOMEONE, CHANGE HIS DIAPERS

Is it possible for love to overcome disgust? Perhaps if you feel deep affection for a person, then he or she is less likely to gross you out. Think about parents! If love weren't stifling a mother's "disgust," she'd run screaming the first time Little Junior smeared poo-poo on the cat.

Still not convinced? To put this notion to the test, Dr. Betty Repacholi had mothers smell different pairs of poopy diapers and then rate their stinkiness. Did the mothers rate their own babies' diapers as less disgusting? Yes! Were the babies' diapers *actually* any less disgusting? Nope!

Oh, rats. I don't have the heart (or stomach!) to actually describe the birth of a baby. So I interviewed a female doctor who specializes in assisting with births. She said, "When I explain to my patients what giving birth is going to be like, I say, 'You'll have every different liquid in your body coming out of every orifice. It's a rainbow of color!'"

Wow, rainbows are pretty! And since there was a lot of pooping on the days that you and I were born, you can probably guess one of the colors of that rainbow. You see, when women have babies, they almost always "void their bowels." So don't act like poop doesn't have anything to do with you. It always has, ever since Day One!

So on everyone's first birthday, there's mucus, blood, poop, pee, body tissues, and a baby all showing up at once! But what does it sound like? Writer Michael Lewis listened to his child being born and described it as "the sound of a hairless dog escaping from quicksand." There is also a lot of screaming.

After the blessed event, there will be more screaming, some green poop, and then a lot of crying. Oh, yes, and green poop. Did I mention that babies make green poop? As a wise man once said, "The only things that should be green are unripe fruits and Martians."

Since I chickened out on describing the delivery, and since this book is about gross stuff, I guess I can't get away without writing about the placenta. This is the lining inside a

WHAT'S THAT KID'S NAME AGAIN?

There are records from the 1700s of a Russian woman named Vassilyev who had 69 children. Keeping track of their birthdays was a little easier than you might guess because all of them shared birthdays! There were:

4 sets of quadruplets (16 kids)

7 sets of triplets (21 kids)

16 pairs of twins (32 kids)

woman's uterus or womb that supplies the nourishment for the baby. The problem is that once the baby is born, the placenta isn't needed anymore. This means that after a baby enters the world, the show's not over! There's still a nutrient-rich sack of flesh (dripping red and gooey) that has to make its appearance. And when it does, you'll know it. (Even if you don't see it yourself, you'll know the placenta has arrived when someone runs out of the delivery room with his hand over his mouth.)

Of course, some women choose to deliver their children at home. And sometimes they do this inside a big tub of warm water. That way the baby doesn't feel such a huge shock coming out of the womb. But since a lot of things like the placenta come out with the baby, the people assisting with the delivery often use tropical fish nets to scoop all the chunks out of the tub's water!

"I'M READY WHEN YOU ARE."

After the delivery of the baby, the placenta is placed with other biowastes for sanitary disposal (whatever that means!). In some cases, though, the placenta will be saved. Why? Because the new parents might want to plant a tree in their child's honor, and the placenta is going to be placed at the bottom of the hole the tree goes into. Or sometimes the parents just want to put the placenta in the freezer for a memento. (Really.)

And SOME parents take the placenta home and make a soup or pâté (cracker spread) out of it. Then they eat it. There might be a way for me to figure out WHY people do this, but I'm too busy throwing up right now to concentrate properly.

BUT I DON'T WANT TO EAT THE BABY!

It is customary in Japan to give new parents a gift. And then the parents give a less valuable gift in return. So a shop in the city of Fukuoka came up with the idea of parents giving out customized bags of rice for their return gifts. The bags are "named" for the new baby and have a photo of the wee one printed on the package. The rice bag even weighs the same as the new family member! Recipients of the gift apparently cuddle the rice baby. Then, later on, they open the baby package and eat its contents.

The Stream of Life

You should be proud. You're the owner of your very own urinary bladder!

"So what?" you ask. Well, your bladder is magic! It can change dramatically in size, going from a flat, deflated little bag (after you pee) to a softball-size balloon when you REALLY have to go. When your bladder is full, it holds about a pint of liquid gold.

You deflate your bladder fairly often. (What a great sentence!) After you pee, you probably remember to wash your hands, right? That's a good idea—except the germs you should worry about are the ones on the bathroom door, NOT

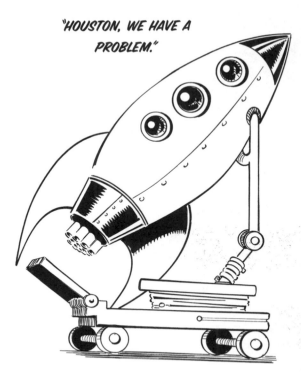

"HOUSTON, WE HAVE A PROBLEM."

the ones in your pee. That's because there aren't any germs in your pee!

Hopefully this made astronaut Alan Shepard feel better about the time he wet his spacesuit. Shepard was the first American ever to travel into outer space. He was also the first to go wee-wee in a rocket. In 1961, Shepard was scheduled to launch on a short flight beyond Earth's atmosphere. But flight delays left the astronaut stuck onboard for longer than planned. Since there was no bathroom for him to use, and he wasn't allowed to get out of his spacesuit, Shepard was finally forced to pee inside it.

TALK ABOUT RUINING A WONDERFUL MOMENT!

After that, spacesuits were designed with urine-collection bags and poop-containment devices. But wetting your spacesuit isn't so bad.[1] In terms of germs, spit is way grosser than pee is. This is weird because you swallow spit,

---

1. Wetting your astronaut pajamas is WAY worse, take it from me! (For one thing, pajamas take longer to dry out.)

but you're not going to drink your own pee. But would you drink someone else's? It's been said that the Chukchi people of Siberia would exchange drinks of urine with new friends and allies. And the Native Americans known as the Zuni used to hold a "urine dance" celebration where they would drink large amounts of pee. (Hey, I think I may have done a urine dance before!)

IF YOU WOULDN'T DRINK THE PEE OF A FRIEND, WHAT ABOUT THE PEE OF A TRUSTED ANIMAL? AFTER ALL, COWS CAN SUPPLY TWO IMPORTANT BEVERAGES TO THIRSTY HUMANS.

1. MILK
2. URINE

You see, cows are greatly respected in India. Millions of people there consider cow urine to be good for the soul. Heck, Mahatma Gandhi drank a cup of the stuff each morning! That's why an Indian group is planning to sell a soft drink made of cow urine. A group official says the drink will be sold as *gau jal*. (This translates to "cow water.")

f your Disgust Meter is now in the yellow, keep in mind that people used to add urine to beer and ale to make it stronger. (This process was called "lanting.") Furthermore, doctors used to taste their patients' pee to check its flavor. If the pee tasted sweet, it was a sign that the patient might have diabetes. And finally, before you were born, you floated for months in fluids that contained your own baby pee!

So what does urine taste like? The crew members of Ferdinand Magellan's 1519 attempt to sail around the world can tell us. The sailors had to drink their own pee after a year and a half at sea. One of them wrote, "It was surprisingly not unsavory, having no worse a taste than a flagon … as many I have tasted before." So maybe it's not so bad! But is your Disgust Meter still in the yellow?

IN ONE END, OUT THE OTHER

Next time you're watching a vampire bat lapping up some blood, you might notice that it's also peeing. That's because vampire bats drink and pee at the same time!

Let's get back to the astronauts. When a NASA shuttle goes into outer space, every pound of its cargo costs a *lot* of money. And water is really heavy! This means that the astronauts' pee is recycled into usable water. You may recall the news story about the three members of the International Space Station drinking their own recycled pee in zero gravity. And for longer missions to Mars, the current plan is to reuse all fluids that come out of the astronauts: from their tears, sweat, breath, *and* pee. (This is sort of like the science-fiction novel *Dune*.)

★ **UNBEPISSED:** Not urinated upon.

If you still think that drinking pee is horrible, I have bad news for you: one of every five people in a swimming pool goes pee in it. And since it's really hard not to get a little water in your mouth when you're swimming, you know what you've done! Sure, it was an *accident*. Tell that to the astronauts!

And now to solve one of the great peeing mysteries of all time! As we know, guys like to pee standing up. They also like to pee onto or into something. So if a man is in a huge field with only one tree really far away, he will usually hike to the tree and pee against it. And if a boy in the desert saw an empty coffee can, he would walk a mile to pee into it. (It makes a funny sound!)

My theory is that this must be an instinct! Researchers have learned that wolves and dogs go out of their way to pee on the most visible and easily smelled spot. (This is especially

true for males.) Male wolves urinate on tall trees, while dogs prefer fire hydrants. Both animals try to aim their pee as high as possible so that the wind will carry the smell even farther. This is what is called "maximum territorial signaling."

When men pee standing up, they are similarly marking their territory. (This sort of peeing sends a fine spray of urine around the room.) To reduce spray, some urinals now come with a mark on them, which men naturally aim at. The mark is put in a spot where pee spray will be reduced. Of course, another simple strategy is to have the man sit down while peeing. While this may sound like no big deal, it presents problems of its own! (See p. 141.)

HOLDING IT

If you're any-thing like me (and I hope you're not!), when you go to a theater to see a movie, it's almost guaranteed that about halfway through you're going to think: "Uh-oh, gotta go!" I guess I should stop chugging liquids before-hand. But instead, I make a point of only going to theaters with thick carpets and absorbent seats. *Kidding!*

But as I squirm and cross my legs, I'm amazed at the other people who can "hold it" for hours and hours. (When will this stupid cartoon end?!) People who can hold it may call themselves "camels," but they should actually call them-selves "bears." That's because when bears hibernate during the winter, they never get up to go pee in the woods. Their body simply reuses the fluids!

★ **PISSUPPREST:** The ability to hold in your urine.

THE COUPLE THAT SPRAYS TOGETHER

When a male porcupine sees a female he's interested in, he sprays her with pee. If the female porcupine stays, she likes him! Now *that's* love.

ROLL OUT THE BARREL

Viking households usually had a barrel full of human pee in the corner. This was used to clean sheep's wool, make soap, and possibly to store food in so that vermin didn't get into it!

But there *is* a time and place to pee your pants. Tycho Brahe (1546–1601) was a famous astronomer from Denmark. He died from pee poisoning after going to a formal dinner. You see, the custom at the time was that guests did not get up from the dinner table until the meal was finished. Apparently, Brahe really had to go, but he refused to leave! As a result, he "held it" too long, and his bladder burst. He died of internal pee poisoning days later.

Kids who wet their beds have the opposite of Brahe's problem. And there are a lot of them! One out of every seven kids is a bed wetter, and 1 percent of all eighteen-year-old boys still wet the bed. If you are ever worried about this, try eating some crackers or having a spoonful of honey before going to bed. Either of these items will help you retain your water. (In ancient Rome, they used to make bed wetters eat boiled mice, so we've come a long way!)

WHERE DOES PEE COME FROM?

Your kidneys are two bean-shaped organs. They are Command Central of your urinary system. Try reaching your hands behind your back and below your rib cage. Now make two fists. This is the approximate size and location of your kidneys! I hope your kidneys are not sleeping on the job, because if they are, you'd be the victim of kidney-napping. (Oh, I am really sorry about that!)

Your blood gets filtered through your kidneys. In fact, a quart of blood gets pushed through them every minute, which is actually pretty amazing. And your kidneys' other important job is keeping track of how much total water you have in your body and getting rid of excess fluids.

About half of your body weight should be water. So your urinary system works with your intestines, lungs, and even your skin to keep those fluids just right. For example, if you're sweating a lot, your urinary system might cut back on the flow of fluid to your urine. Your kidneys also keep tabs on your waste, salt, and sugar levels.

From your kidneys, pee travels directly to your urinary bladder. As your bladder fills, circular, rubber band-like muscles (called sphincters) tighten up so that it doesn't leak. You can control these muscles. When you're ready, you can relax those bladder sphincters, which releases pee to the bladder's "exit," a tube called the urethra. This tube then delivers your pee to, um, the outside world.

Yay.

THE #1 TAX

All sorts of things have been taxed over the years, like candy bars, gasoline, and even beards. (Really!) But the Roman emperor Nero was the only person to put a tax on pee.

About two thousand years ago, Roman tanners collected pee from public restrooms. That's because the ammonia in pee could be used for things like laundry bleach. And since the pee could be had for free, but the tanners charged a fee to bleach people's laundry, Nero decided to take a cut of the pee-pee action!

So what ends up in your pee? Water. Unused vitamins. Salt. Waste proteins. One particular waste that is removed from your blood is called urea. Urea is sort of a weird substance. Once it sits around, urea breaks down into ammonia, which stinks but can be good for cleaning things. Urea is often found in lotions because it's supposedly good for curing acne and other skin conditions. (An old Mexican custom was to use a boy's warm urine on skin rashes!)

Pee can have a number of different colors. For example, I was once convinced that I was peeing blood because my pee had a strong rusty color to it. Not to worry! It turns out that the beets I had eaten the night before were staining my urine. And vitamin B will give your pee a bright yellow color. If your pee is a dark brownish-yellow color, you need to drink more water. Your body needs lots of clear fluids to flush itself out properly, and really dark urine can be a sign of dehydration.

As for stinky pee, nothing beats asparagus. And while it can take hours for the red color of beets to get into your urine, the asparagus smell seems to happen in just an hour or so. Awesome!

Before I end this chapter, let me give you some free medical advice: If you're ever in a hospital, don't drink anything that looks like apple juice. Thank you, and good night.

ANIMALS!

As a person who loves animals, I'd like to point out that no animals are gross. It is only our reactions to our fellow creatures that make them *seem* gross.

This is very childish on our part!

Take the candiru, for example. It's a wee South American catfish that looks like a five-inch-long eel. It likes nothing better than minding its own business. Sure, the candiru feasts on the blood and soft tissues of other fish by swimming into their gills. But who are we to judge?

One scientist studying the candiru learned just how much it likes blood. The scientist was standing in a river, and the fishy dove into a little cut in his skin, burrowed into it, and headed for an artery. This scared the heck out of the scientist, who managed to stop the little troublemaker before it swam into his heart. Okay, I'll admit it, that *is* pretty bad. But wait, it's not as frightening as something I just heard about. Apparently, a man was peeing into the Amazon River when a candiru swam up his urine stream and … made a home in the place the urine was coming out of. *Ulp.* It was days before a surgeon was able to get the fish out. The man survived, but the candiru ended up doing some traveling inside him before everything was said and done.

WHAT HORRIBLE LITTLE BEASTS! KILL THEM ALL!

Whew, I'm sorry! I got a little spooked there. As I said before, animals cannot be disgusting. To prove it, I'm visiting the zoo right now. (They let me bring my typewriter inside!) I asked the zookeeper to direct me to the most allegedly gross animal. And so even as I write, I'm looking at an African rodent called the naked mole rat. *Ha!* Only an uptight human could look at an innocent creature and call it "naked." All animals are naked.

And so what if the only hair a naked mole rat has is … in its mouth. And big deal if baby naked mole rats have pink skin that's so transparent I can actually see all of their internal organs pulsing inside of them.

Blech! (Dang it, I just dropped my typewriter!)

I guess animals *can* be disgusting— just like us! Here are some notables:

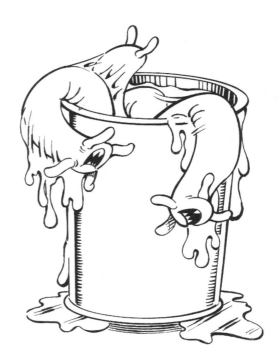

SLIMIEST OF THE SLIMY AWARD WINNER: The slime eel is such an overachiever, it even has a charming nickname: "hagfish." But whatever you call this fish, it's covered in mucus. It has ninety pores on its body that produce slime!

But the slime eel's slime isn't just any slime. As the slime comes out of the eel's body, it has the consistency of a horrible gelatin. If you were to get some of it on you, washing it off wouldn't work. The more water comes into contact with it, the thicker and slimier the slime gets! Apparently, the best solution is to *peel* it off.

As if that weren't enough, the slime eel also has lips with tentacles attached to them! It swims along the bottom of the sea floor and looks for fish that are either dead or sick.

It then goes in the fish's mouth (or gill or eye or butt) and eats the fish from the inside out. How? It uses its tooth-covered tongue to scrape the fish to pieces. Oh, and it gets a bonus score for being made up entirely of intestine. The slime eel has no stomach—and four hearts! And it doesn't have any bones, either. Good grief, is this thing even from our planet?

UNDERTAKER PRIZE: The burial beetle, also known as the carrion beetle, looks like an oversized ladybug. But it doesn't fly away home. Instead, it comes out at night and starts looking for dead rodents or birds. When it finds one, the beetle crawls all over the carcass, leaving behind anti-fungal juices. This slows the rotting process. By keeping the stink down, the burial beetle improves its chances at not having to share with other scavengers!

Then the beetle digs under the corpse until the rodent or bird slowly sinks into the ground. This might take all night, and by the time the sun has come up, the beetle can start chowing down and laying eggs. When the beetle's larvae hatch, it thoughtfully bites off chunks of the carcass and then barfs them back up for the babies to eat!

MOST DISGUSTING WAY TO SAY "I LOVE YOU" PRIZE: The anglerfish is one ugly denizen of the deep. It has a stalk coming out of its head with a glowing light at the end of it. This is how it attracts prey to its huge jaws and colossal teeth.

At least that's what female anglerfish do. The males are much smaller than the females, and they don't live long. As soon as a male anglerfish is fully grown, his digestive system dissolves! So his job is to find a female anglerfish, and fast. *Look, over there, a light!* Then the male has to swim over and bite the female on the side. *Don't let go!* He has to keep biting and burrowing into her skin until all that's left of him is his back half sticking out of her side. Then he stays put! His head and the front half of his body eventually disintegrate inside the female. Older female anglerfish can have more than seven males sticking out of their body. (If that's what love is, I don't want any part of it!)

BEST ANIMAL TO WALK WITH ON A COLD DAY: Besides their drool and vomit, dogs aren't gross in the slightest.

And they can even keep your hands warm on a cold day! You see, dogs have an interior temperature of 101 degrees Fahrenheit. That's pretty warm. Let's say that you're out walking Fido on a cold morning and you've forgotten your gloves. Don't despair! After Fido busts a grumpy, just bag it and then put it in your pocket. Now you have your very own hand warmer!

But don't forget to get rid of that bag before hanging up your coat.

MOST HORRIBLE WAY TO BE BORN AWARD WINNER:
Would you like being born in a blister? That's how little baby Surinam toads come into the world. Here's how it works:

A female Surinam toad releases her eggs into water, where the male fertilizes them. Using toad acrobatics, the female manages to get about a hundred of the fertilized eggs onto her back. And there they stay!

THE BIG HORSE APPLE

In the 1970s, New York City became the first major city to require dog owners to clean up their dogs' poop.

Over the next few hours, the eggs nest into the female's back, and a layer of skin forms over them. Then during the next few weeks, little toad tadpoles hatch within these bubbles. When they're ready, the baby Surinam hoppers break free of their bubbles and launch themselves into the world. (Hey, if one female toad met another female toad from the same mother, it could say, "You're my sister from another blister!")

And Mom is left with a back covered with popped blisters.

MOST DISGUSTING BABIES PRIZE: The female Australian social spider gives birth to many babies at once. Unlike other spiders, she then lets her babies suck her juices out. Then the little brats puke all over her and eat the dissolved mess.

WEIRDEST WAY TO EAT CHAMPION: A starfish actually upchucks its stomach onto the things it wants to eat. This releases digestive juices right on the food. Then the starfish swallows its stomach, slurping down the liquefied food right along with it!

"DAM RODENTS" PRIZE: Beavers are sort of cute, and very industrious. But they can have an intestinal parasite called giardia. Also nicknamed "beaver fever," giardia is the second-leading waterborne disease in the United States. If a human gets giardia, it can mean diarrhea, and lots of it. So if you're backpacking in beaver country, remember to boil your water. If you don't, you're going to need the beavers to build a dam behind your butt!

THE MOST WELL-DEVELOPED ANAL GLANDS IN THE WORLD AWARD: A skunk has anal sacs that are filled with extremely stinky fluid. And it can shoot this fluid a long way. But incredibly, the skunk doesn't win this award. Instead, it goes to an African animal called the zorilla. The zorilla actually looks like a skunk, but it smells even worse. A famous zoologist said that it has the "most well-developed anal glands in the animal kingdom." The stink of a zorilla's anal gland is so bad, these animals don't even hang out with each other!

NEITHER PLANT NOR ANIMAL

For the record, there are five "kingdoms" of life: plant, animal, fungi, bacteria, and ... slime mold! A slime mold is neither a plant nor an animal. So what is it? One scientist called slime mold "a bag of amoebas."

SLIME TIME

Here's a slimy activity:

Build a maze and put some delicious spores and bacteria at one end. (Don't eat them yourself—they're for the slime mold!)

Now get a slime mold. (Your local pet store probably has some. Or not. But you really can order slime mold growth kits from most biological supply houses.) Carefully cut the slime mold into pieces and drop them into the maze. (Don't worry, this doesn't hurt the slime mold.)

Watch as the slime mold parts put themselves back together again. Now watch as the original slime mold starts to move through the maze! See how it learns to avoid dead ends? Notice how it heads for those delicious spores? See how the now-larger slime mold picks up the knife you used to cut it up with and—*Eeep!*[1]

1. All of this is true except the knife part.

While there are more than a thousand slime mold species, nearly all begin life as an innocent little oatmeal-like glob that oozes around the forest floor, engulfing the bacteria it finds in rotting wood. This organism is also sometimes called "dog vomit mold" because people who come upon it in their backyards assume that their dog just blew chunks. Amazing!

Even more amazing, I have it on good authority that people in some parts of Mexico collect certain slime molds. Then they make a scramble of them in a pan, like eggs. The dish is called *caca de luna*, which translates to "poop of the moon"!

FUN(GUS) FACTS!

The ancient Romans had a lot of gods, and one of them was Robigus, Lord of Fungus! Robigus was also the easygoing god of farms and fertility. But after a cruel Roman kid set a fox's tail on fire, Robigus decided to give wheat crops a horrible fungus called "wheat rust." This fungus ruined the wheat for humans, and foxes rejoiced.

You and I actually have a lot in common with the fungus world. We are all *opisthokonts*. That means we can't make food with our bodies like a plant can. Instead, we have to eat something else ... like wheat!

WHILE WE HUMANS EAT FOOD BY STICKING IT INSIDE OUR BODIES AND DIGESTING IT, FUNGI DO THE OPPO-SITE. THEY GRAB ONTO A FOOD AND RELEASE ENZYMES ON IT TO BREAK IT DOWN. THEN THE FUNGI ABSORB THE FOOD THROUGH THEIR MEMBRANES. THAT'S RIGHT, FUNGI ABSORB. WEIRD, HUH?

Fungi are nature's decomposers. They eat some living things and almost all dead ones. Heck, they even feed on stuff that never lived at all! Fungi chow down on things like bread, wood, bananas, cloth, leather, sponges, dead humans, and even plastic and paint. They're unstoppable! Cold temperatures don't really bother most fungi, so if you leave cottage cheese in the refrigerator or in the freezer, even these food items will eventually get moldy! (Mold is just another fungus.)

Instead of using seeds to reproduce, fungi use spores. These tiny reproductive cells are floating all around us. And if a fungal spore lands on something that might possibly be "food," then fungus will grow there. In fact, your body is constantly fighting the little fungus spores trying to grow in your lungs. Luckily, your immune system does this pretty easily. But patients going through chemotherapy have weaker immune systems than most healthy people. This can create an opening for a fungus called *Aspergillus fumigatus*. Once this fungus infects the lungs, it kills almost 90 percent of its victims!

A less deadly but still disgusting fungus is the little stink-horn. This is a fungus that eats rotting wood. Once a stink-horn spore lands on a likely spot, it will grow a stalk several inches tall with an oozing ball at the top. This ball smells like rotting meat! This attracts insects, which land on the ball, where they become coated in the stinkhorn's gooey spores. Then the bugs fly off.

AND THAT'S HOW THE LITTLE STINKHORN GETS AROUND!

An even more fascinating travel tale comes to us from truffles. A truffle is a fungus that grows underneath rich woodland soil. Besides being covered in dirt, truffles are pretty ugly; they look sort of like fungus meteorites with a thick bumpy skin. Some humans claim to like the truffle's taste, and they're willing to pay top dollar for them. Italian white truffles are going for $4,000 a pound right now!

What's odd about this is that a truffle is mostly made up of fungal spores, and animals (humans included) can't digest fungal spores! So a person eats a truffle and poops the truffle's spores out. This is sort of a waste, since most humans flush their poop instead of going out and taking a dump on the woodland floor. If more truffle-eaters would poop in the woods, there would be more truffles. (And then everyone could afford them!)

STOMACH-CHURNING WORMS

My curiosity about worms began at an early age. I was often told that "the worms crawl in, the worms crawl out." But what goopy mischief are they doing between entering and exiting?

In the case of the giant sea worm, they're making a *lot* of mischief. Recently, the workers at a big British aquarium were really confused. One of their colossal tanks had a vandal, but they couldn't figure out who (or what) was injuring its fish and destroying its coral. So at night, workers would lay bait traps set with fish hooks. But in the morning, the traps would be gone, fish hooks and all!

Eventually, the staff spotted a four-foot-long sea worm. It was a truly frightening worm, bristling with spikes and a mouth that would make you shudder. Marine biologists warned that if anyone were stung by the beast, it would cause permanent numbness. Man, that was one scary worm! To catch it, they fed the creature bait attached to a fishing line. The worm promptly ate the bait ... and bit through the line! No one knew what the beast was doing there, but they guessed that a sea worm larva or egg may have snuck into the aquarium when another marine animal was introduced.

To get the horrible-looking, spiny beast out, they drained the aquarium and did the only thing they could do: they put the worm in his own aquarium. Then they named it "Barry"!

IT TURNS OUT THAT THE OCEAN HAS A NUMBER OF DISGUSTING CREATURES, AND ONE OF THE WORST IS THE SACCULINA. IT'S SORT OF A COMBINATION OF A VAMPIRE, A ZOMBIE SCIENTIST ... AND A BARNACLE.

Let me explain!

A baby sacculina is a tiny creature related to the barnacle. It floats happily along in the water until it sees a nice crab to infect. Once a crab is located, the sacculina drills itself right into the crab's body, where it starts eating its flesh and

getting bigger. Tendrils grow out of the sacculina and into the crab's body. Pretty soon, the parasite's tendrils reach from stem to stern. The poor crab is now the sacculina's zombie, existing only to eat and provide a home for the creature as it mates, has baby sacculinas, and then takes over other crabs.

So if you ever open crack a crab and find a parasite's tentacles inside it, now you know what you're up against!

While these examples are revolting, probably the most unpleasant place to find a parasitic worm (or "gut nematode") is inside *you*. Take the tapeworm, for example. Any animal that eats meat might also eat the eggs or larvae of one of the species of tapeworm. But don't worry, you probably won't get one of these worms unless you ever happen to eat pork, fish, or beef.

ONCE A TAPEWORM IS INSIDE YOUR SYSTEM, IT FINDS A SPOT DEEP WITHIN YOUR SMALL INTESTINE TO SET UP SHOP. THEN THE TAPEWORM ANCHORS ITSELF. HOW? WELL, IT HAS A BIG SUCKER ON ITS HEAD, AND IT HAS HOOKS TOO. (YEAH, I GUESS YOU WERE BETTER OFF NOT KNOWING.)

The tapeworm feeds on the food passing by, and it starts to grow. The key to understanding how big a tapeworm gets is to think about how your intestines wind around and around inside your body, sort of like a coiled rope. As the tapeworm gets longer, it also coils around inside you. It can grow up to thirty feet long!

As the tapeworm gets bigger, it grows segments that are full of thousands of eggs. These segments look like flat pieces of tape, and they eventually break off and exit your body along with your poop. The idea is that the eggs will find a new home inside another lucky host somewhere else.

If the tapeworm is too big to think about, try the fluke on for size. These little flatworms are so small that they can sneak into your body right through your skin. Next stop? Your liver, where the flukes will lay millions of eggs and start swimming all through your bloodstream!

Pinworms are also very gross. These tiny little creatures live inside people's butts. (Kids usually get pinworms, because pinworm larvae are found in the dirt, and kids both play in dirt and do a crummy job washing their hands.) At night, the pinworms come out of their, uh, home and lay their eggs in butt cheek land. How does a person know he or she has pinworms? Can you say "itchy"?

Roundworms look the most like earthworms of any of our parasites. These worms are supposed to hang out in the intestines, but they are sort of like nomads, traveling throughout the body. They have been known to suddenly show up in a person's nose, mouth, or anus.

And that is very uncool.

But of all the disgusting worms I know of, I think the worst is the hookworm. Hookworms are about a half-inch long, and they like nothing better than hanging out in poop and dirt and then burrowing into the soles of people who are walking around barefoot. From there, it's on to the intestines, where the hookworms latch on and start gorging on blood and reproducing. What do the baby hookworms do? Latch on, gorge on blood, and reproduce! And since hookworms may be in as many as one in four people worldwide, they're doing a pretty good job of it. But a good job for a hookworm is a bad thing for a human. In extreme cases of hookworm infection, the victim loses so much blood he turns pale, becomes weak and tired, and can start suffering heart problems. The victim's hair may even change color!

Some people think earthworms are gross, but that's silly. They're harmless! However, a relative of the earthworm is definitely bad news. Yep, I'm talking about the leech. While earthworms don't bite, a leech can bite you twice at the same time! That's because many leeches have two mouths. Leeches find this handy, since a lot of them want to suck your blood. But leech bites are painless. After cutting through your skin with its sharp teeth, the leech quickly spits into the bite. And since leech spit kills pain, you probably won't notice the bite at all.

In addition to having two mouths, the leech also has two suckers, one at each end. One sucker has the two mouths at the center, and the other sucker has the leech's anus in the middle. So that's what you call a "lose-lose" sucker situation.

There are hundreds of kinds of leeches, and luckily, some of them prefer eating garbage. Some leeches even attach themselves to dead animals, so they are NOT choosy! They range in size from tiny to over two feet long. Leeches may clamp onto your legs, but they also like to swim to a dark

CHIGGERS ARE (NOT) WONDERFUL THINGS

Chiggers are little mites that dig into the skin of animals, especially during the summer. The little buggers inject a fluid into the skin that liquefies a tiny portion of it. Then the chigger eats this dissolved skin. Little jerk! This inflames the surrounding skin and leaves a red welt that itches like crazy. Since the chigger is red too, this makes the tiny demon hard to spot and explains why almost everyone hates chiggers.

crevice where you won't find them, like your armpit, your butt, or worse! No, I did not make that up. These types of leeches are usually found in Africa, Asia, and islands in the Pacific and Indian oceans.

If you're in blood-sucking leech country and you find a leech on you, don't cut it off. You could cut that leech right in half and it would keep sucking! In the movies, adventurers often put the lit end of a cigarette on the leech to make it let go. But since you don't smoke, this won't work. (Dang, the *one* thing smoking is good for!) Instead, put salt or lemon juice on the leech. Then it will let go. (Ice cubes also work, but since you'd probably be out in a tropical rain forest if you got a leech, I'm guessing you won't have an ice cube on you!)

The worst leech story I've heard is this one: An Australian woman was out gardening when she accidentally got some soil in her eye ... and a small leech was in there too. The leech started feasting on the blood from her eyeball! Even though she got medical attention, the leech quickly tripled in size. Nasty!

So how did the doctors get rid of this eyeball-sucking monster? By giving her some eye drops of saline solution! As one doctor reported, "The leech rolled straight off, it just fell onto her cheek, so we put it in a pot and gave it to her."

Gee, thanks, Doc!

BREAKING THE WIND

Hot air rises. That makes having gas—or "flatulence"—
one of this book's lighter topics! And since both the
ancient Greeks and Romans thought that "breaking
the wind" was amusing, it also has a time-honored place in
entertainment.

Today, flatulence still has the power to make some people
laugh, and Trevor Cox is one of them. Cox is a professor of
acoustics who is doing research on the sound of flatulence.
As part of his research, he conducted a series of experi-
ments to find out what kind of farting sounds would be rated
as the funniest by listeners.

Cox's theory is that people will laugh the most at an unexpectedly odd farting sound. This proved true for me; I took part in the experiment, and I thought the *"Phfwwoothf"* fart was a riot. (Who'd ever heard of such a thing!)

Unlike burping, there are no places where it's polite to pass gas. In fact, it can get you into trouble! An eighth grader in Lakeland, Florida, was suspended from riding the bus for passing too much gas. And a British soccer referee once gave a yellow penalty card to a whole soccer team because one of its players farted loudly during its opponent's penalty kick. The charge was "ungentlemanly conduct." (Hard to argue with that!)

People obviously have very strong feelings about flatulence. In the 1880s, British explorer Richard Burton explained how in the Middle East, people burped to show that they were enjoying their food. But he added that the desert nomads had a "mortal hatred" of

THE SMELLER'S THE FELLER

A Scottish man named Stewart Laidlaw was banned from his local pub for "basking in the glory of his smells." Of course, Laidlaw made the mistake of taking credit for the smells he was basking in!

NOM DE FUMES

Flatus (FLAY-tus) is the scientific term for bodily gas. But there are hundreds of other fantastic words and phrases you can use when you've got to "drop a bomb." Here are some possibilities:

bowel howl

right-cheek sneak

roll of thunder, hear my cry

letting the air out of my tires

backfire

hot boxing (deliberately closing the windows in a room before farting)

Dutch oven (farting under the sheets)

breaking some bad news

ponging

stepping on a mud cricket

trouser cough

thunder down under

playing the butt bongos

wind beneath my wings

breaking the sound barrier

trumping (British)

the butler's revenge (British)

having the vapors (Victorian)

flatulence, and if someone were to accidentally bomb and then laugh, "he would be cut down at once."

Here are some even more alarming incidents from the "bombs away" Hall of Shame:

★ In 569 BCE, King Apries of Egypt sent an envoy to a rebellious general named Amasis. When Amasis met the king's envoy, he passed gas and then told the envoy to carry that message back to the king.

The envoy did so! We don't know if he just reported "Amasis farted" or if the envoy actually tried to repeat the message "word for word." But we do know that King Apries got so mad that he had the envoy's nose and ears cut off. This was so cruel and unfair that popular support swung to Amasis. The rebel general ended up ruling Egypt from 569 to 525 BCE! (As for King Apries, he was eventually killed by an angry mob.)

★ In 44 CE, a Roman soldier in Jerusalem loudly and intentionally passed gas near Jews observing Passover. In the following riot, ten thousand people died.

★ Sir Thomas More wrote in 1518, "Wind, if you keep it too long . . . kills you; on the other hand, it can save your life if properly let out. If wind can save or destroy you, then is it not as powerful as dreaded kings?" (He was later beheaded by order of King Henry VIII.)

★ In the 1600s, an explorer on Africa's Gambia River noted that the Ashanti people viewed flatulence as so horrible, one man hung himself after he accidentally "let one" while bowing to a chief!

★ In 1943, Adolf Hitler's doctor noted that the German dictator had "colossal flatulence . . . on a scale I have seldom encountered before." (And the papers of a high-ranking Nazi officer that were unearthed in the twenty-first century confirmed Der Führer's gassiness.) So, in addition to having bad table manners and biting his nails, Hitler stank.

★ In 2003, Nickelodeon debuted a new award at its Kids' Choice Awards: "Favorite Fart in a Movie." The winner was Scooby Doo.

At the moment, you have about a quart of gas bottled up inside you (everyone does!), and it's only a matter of time before it works its way out as a burp or flatulence. But where does your gas actually come from? Why, I'm glad you asked!

YOU HAVE THE RIGHT TO REMAIN SILENT BUT DEADLY

There are hordes of bacteria living in your small and large intestines. Don't freak out—they're doing an important job! These bacteria break down the food moving through your guts. As the bacteria feed on the food that your body has trouble breaking down (like bran), they make tiny amounts of stinky chemicals called *indole* and *skatole*. The organisms then release these substances in the form of gas. (Those little jerks!)

So basically, it isn't you that's farting, it's your bacteria. Even though only about 1 percent of your farts stink, that 1 percent can be horrible! What makes them stink? Well, for starters, it isn't exactly helpful that they come out of your butt. And they contain hydrogen sulfide, which has that rotten-egg smell. Definitely stinky! The types of food you eat and the kinds of bacteria you have in your intestines also determine how much of a gas called *methane* you have in your bombs. If your intestines have a lot of methane, your farts are going to run hot and silent (otherwise known as "Silent But Deadly").

Methane is flammable, so farts with a lot of methane can catch fire and even explode! (Only about a third of all people can produce enough methane to make this work.) Much, much worse than this are the rare occasions where medical surgeons have opened up a patient's guts and released

The Seven Commandments of Farting

He who smelt it, dealt it.

He who hot boxed it should detox it.

He who rejected it, ejected it.

He who denied it, refried it.

He who contradicts it made the butt bongo mix for it.

He who disowned it should atone for it.

He who declined it, land-mined it.

methane gas. If anything sparks in the operating room while they do so (like some high-tech electronics or a Boy Scout trying to start a fire in the corner), the patient's guts will explode!

That's what we call "Not Very Silent and Pretty Darned Deadly."

Whatever the source, if you feel the need to let some gas out, be careful. Very careful! You see, your sphincter is in charge of both pooping and letting gas out. So it's *very* important that your sphincter doesn't confuse one for the other!

GOOD NEWS!

Your sphincter is pretty good at telling the difference between solid poop and gas. Without it, you'd potentially poop your pants every time you passed gas.

BAD NEWS!

Your sphincter is *not* very good at telling the difference between liquid poop and gas. So if you have diarrhea, and you think you need to pass gas, you might want to go to the bathroom. Do not tempt fate! You've heard the old expression "Where there's smoke, there's fire"? Well, where there's gas, there's feces. And if you gamble and lose, you're going to be REALLY unhappy!

Any way you look at it, you're going to have gas. If you prefer to hold it in, that's fine, but it will come out eventually. And then it will reek even more! How big, long, and stinky your bombs are depends on how long you've been holding them in and what you've been eating. While everyone's body reacts to food in different ways, there are definitely some choice items that will get your bacteria percolating:

FOOD	SOUND	REACTION FROM OTHERS
red meat	Flubbety	"Why? Why? Why?"
beans	Plbbp!	"Now do you feel at home?"
bell peppers	Flomp	"I think you just sat on a chair rat."
broccoli	Pooooot	"Are you okay?"
Brussels sprouts	Phlunk	"Something seems to have crawled into your colon and died."
cabbage	Schlank!	"Did an outhouse just explode?"
cauliflower	Proodle-proodle	"Sniff lightly and let it get around."
cheese	Shlufferj	"Your voice has changed, but your breath remains the same."
eggs	Tup-tup-blert!	"Bring it up again and we'll vote on it."
garlic	Gwaack!	"Huh?"
greasy, fried foods	Fffffffft!	"Is something on the stove?"
mushrooms	Weeee-ohhh-whip	"There appear to be gnomes underfoot."
onions	Herrrrkle	"Are you wearing bug spray?"
pears	Pop-pop . . . uh-oh	"Where's my inhaler?"
prunes	Shiggety burple	"Oh yeah?"
raisins	Tut-tuttle-toop!	"Mommy!"
whole wheat	Freep	"Home-brewed!"

If you want to decrease your own gas, try to avoid eating large amounts of these foods. Another possibility is making use of commercial products like the one named "Subtle Butt." This comes in the form of two adhesive strips that you stick inside your underwear. Subtle Butt will then trap and eliminate the odor from any pongs or butt bongos. (It will not muffle sound, however.) Three cheers for "discreet antimicrobial carbon technology"! (Okay, how about two?)

FLATULISTS AND FARTISTES

In the 1770s, a Japanese performer known as the Mist-Descending Flower-Blossom Man entertained audiences by imitating dog barks, a water mill, and fireworks. He did this by passing gas! Yep, the Mist-Descending Flower-Blossom Man bombed loudly, and he achieved different sounds and notes while doing so. Incredible!

But there has never been a "fartiste" quite like French stage performer Joseph Pujol (1857–1945), otherwise known as *Le Pétomane:* the Fart-o-maniac. As a child, Pujol found that he had the rare ability to bring in air through his rear end. He could then let the air back out and make sounds while doing so. (This meant he had to be careful swimming. The problem was that the water would go into his back end, and he would begin to sink!)

In other words, Pujol could make butt bongos any time he wanted to, and they didn't smell! He began working on a nightclub act. Pujol could bomb in many different sounds and for incredible lengths of time. Some of his imitations included cannons, thunder, dogs, birds (including ducks and owls), bees, frogs, and pigs. He could also use his bombs to imitate the sound of someone talking or playing a flute. To close his show, he would blow out a candle!

To offset his earthy performance, Pujol wore an elegant suit onstage. Maybe that was the important touch! People

FLATULENCE SOLVES ANOTHER CRIME!

In 2009, Danish police traced a criminal to a house in Jutland. Police officers entered the house, but they had difficulty finding the elusive criminal. Finally, a horrible smell led them to a closet, where they found the man hiding under a pile of clothes. "It was probably the excitement that caused him to pass wind, and it was the smell that led us to the man," said the chief inspector.

laughed so hard that they sometimes had to be carried out by nurses. Pujol almost always got a standing ovation. During his peak, he earned more money per performance than any other entertainer in Paris.

Pujol's modern successor is Paul Oldfied, aka, The Prince of Poots, aka, Mr. Methane. Gifted with the ability to bring air in and out of his backdoor, he's able to play a number of tunes, including "Smoke on the Water" and "Flight of the Bumblebee." (Legal trouble stopped him from performing

LEAVE IT TO THE PROS

Maybe it's just because they're bigger and as a result produce more gas, but professional athletes are legendary for having bad bombs. When basketball player Zach Randolph was a member of the Portland Trailblazers, his flatulence was so horrible that it could stop practice. And Raef LaFrentz was even worse. The crimes he committed while the team flew to road games led Trailblazer star Brandon Roy to claim he was about ready to "jump out of that plane."

the Phil Collins song "In the Air Tonight.") At six feet and seven inches in height, Oldfield "cuts" a commanding figure onstage!

ANIMAL PERFORMANCES

Herring have been around for ages, but it wasn't until recently that anyone noticed these fish pass gas—in the form of bubbles! Researchers found that herring apparently only bomb in darkened water, and they do so to communicate their positions with each other. Passing gas keeps a school of herring together!

Gas serves an opposite use for coral snakes in the American Southwest. The Sonoran coral snake can release compressed air in loud pops to warn away other animals. It's sort of like a flatulent rattlesnake, without the rattle!

Unsurprisingly, whales have the most gigantic bombs of any animal. But if you compare the size of the animal with its gas output, termites take the cake. Termite gas is actually impacting global warming! (For every human on the planet, there are more than a thousand pounds of termites.)

CAUTION
BOMB
ZONE

Turtles usually get the nod for having the stinkiest bombs, and the loudest bomber in the animal kingdom is the donkey. The donkey's relative, the horse, got saddled with one of the worst names related to this subject. You see, a number of racehorses have been named "Hoof-Hearted" (say it fast!) by their owners. (That is sooo immature.)

THE POWER OF TECHNOLOGY

Back in the Middle Ages, court jesters were known to inflate pig bladders to make farting sounds. But times have changed, and today we use iPhones instead. That's progress!

As you know, the iPhone can be loaded up with all sorts of mini-applications. And some of the most popular mini-apps are the ones that use the iPhone to make farting sounds. As of this writing, there are seventy-five of these programs. There are no doubt a number of people who've bought an iPhone just to have a high-tech Whoopee cushion.

The application called the iFart Mobile makes sounds called Burrito Maximo, Jack the Ripper, and Brown Mosquito. It was the number-one selling iPhone application for a long time!

THE NOSE THAT KNOWS

Many household appliances run on something called natural gas. This type of gas has no smell at all! But that can be dangerous. What if the gas to the oven was turned on without a flame? Natural gas would fill the house, which could lead to explosions, deaths, and mayhem. (And it might make someone spill his prune juice.)

To avoid this problem, the gas company adds a tiny amount of a certain odor to natural gas. The smell is called methyl mercaptan, which is a fancy way of saying it smells like rotting meat. And that definitely gets people's attention!

During that time, the second-best-selling fart application was called Pull My Finger (made by a company called Air-O-Matic). Since Air-O-Matic thought it had the copyright on the phrase "pull my finger," it took legal action against the makers of iFart when they used the phrase in a marketing campaign.

I'm not pulling your leg. Air-O-Matic thinks it owns "pull my finger"! In protest over this stupidity, I'm going to hold out for a mini-application that is REALLY realistic, like the iStink.

If you don't want to hassle with mini-applications, get a balloon instead. Now get out a funnel, some vinegar, and a box of baking soda. Since you're finding all these supplies in the kitchen, set up by the sink. Using the funnel, get about a quarter cup of baking soda in the balloon. Now pour a bit of vinegar in and squeeze the balloon's neck closed. Let the gas build up inside, and then gently open the balloon's neck a bit. Experiment for optimal disgustingness.

★ **BORBORYGMUS:** The rumbling, gurgling noise that gas and fluids make in your intestines. "Dude, I didn't bomb. That was merely borborygmus."

BURPING, BELCHING, AND ERUCTATION

Your skin can burp. Criss Angel told me so!

The magician had eight giant fish hooks embedded in the skin on his back and legs. The hooks were attached to cords. These were then lifted up, and Angel hung from the hooks for a few hours.

Don't ask me why he did this. It's entertainment! (I guess.)

Anyway, after Angel finished the stunt, the hooks had to come back out of his skin. But since the skin had been pulled pretty hard, there were air pockets below the eight spots where he'd been hooked. These spots had to be massaged until the air "burped" out, often with a nice little explosion of blood to go with it!

But the burping that most of us are familiar with comes from excess gas in the stomach rising through the esophagus and mouth. (This is also known as *eructation* and *aerophagia*.) How can air make all that noise? Ah, that's the epiglottis—the flap of skin and cartilage that covers your windpipe so that you don't breathe in food or liquids. (It's also responsible for making the "hiccup" sound when you hiccup.) So, when rising air makes your epiglottis start flopping around, the sound effect can be impressive!

FREE FALLIN'

One good thing to have when you burp is gravity. This allows only air to come up from your stomach. Astronauts in zero gravity NEVER burp. Since there's no gravity, if they burp, everything in their stomach might come up at once!

People consider belches gross because nobody wants to hear a flapping epiglottis. And some animals feel the same way. Orangutans use loud belches to warn away intruders. These apes know that when you belch, you're often bringing up some nasty smells from your guts. And it's even possible for you to burp too violently and then barf your guts up!

Okay, I guess that last one is pretty unlikely.

MONSTERS!

You know, I've seen quite a few gross monster movies in my time. But there is one particular film that sticks out in my mind like an amputated thumb. It was a zombie movie that I stayed up late to watch.

By myself.

The house was dark and silent, except for the screams coming from the television and the whimpers coming from me. (Admittedly, I was probably too young to be watching this film.[1]) The worst part was when one of the zombies leaned

---

1.   I had just celebrated my 31st birthday.

forward and took a bite out of someone's neck like it was a calzone.

Man, that was nasty! But while I was thoroughly disgusted, I was also able to laugh a little, both at myself for being such a coward and also because I remembered some of my favorite zombie jokes.

WHAT DO ZOMBIES EAT?
Braaaains.

WHAT DO VEGETARIAN ZOMBIES EAT?
Graaaains.

WHY DID THE ZOMBIE CROSS THE ROAD?
Braaaains.

ZOMBIES AT A PROTEST:
"What do we want?"
"*Braaaains!*"
"When do we want it?"
"*Braaaains!*"

HOW MANY ZOMBIES DOES IT TAKE TO CHANGE A LIGHTBULB?
Braaaains.

"KNOCK KNOCK."

"Who's there?"

"Zombie."

"Zombie who?"

"Braaaains!"

A ZOMBIE, A PRIEST, AND A RABBI ARE IN A ROWBOAT—

Braaaaaaains!

Of course, humans invented (and discovered!) all sorts of monsters before movies came out. These creatures ranged from uncanny (BANSHEES) to creepy (VAMPIRES) to old-school gruesome (WEREWOLVES). And then there are the creatures of the night that seem to get most of their power just from being gross.

The Japanese have a monster tradition that goes *way* back. Together, these old-time Japanese monsters are known as the *yokai*—"the otherworldly." One of the more disgusting *yokai* is the *akaname*, or "filth licker." He eats bathtub scum. Yep, he shows up in the bathroom and licks mildew. That's his "monstrous" behavior! But if an akaname shows up in a Japanese house to feast, it really is horrible. That's because people in Japan take clean bathrooms very seriously!

Another member of the *yokai* is the *onibaba*, or "demon hag." She's a horrible old woman who collects baby livers.

Talk about bad habits! Today, there's a theme park in Japan near the ancestral "home" of the onibaba. And one of the park's mascots is Bappy-chan, who seems to be a cute little-kid version of the onibaba! ("Welcome to our theme park! Admission is two thousand yen, or one baby liver.")

But don't get the idea that the Japanese have a gross monster monopoly. From the icy forests of Finland comes the legend of the *ovda*. This creature only approaches people in the deep woods. It looks just like a human; the only clue that it's a monster is its feet, which point backward. After the dreadful monster gets to you, it will start tickling you. To death! This may be a weird way of tenderizing your meat, because then the ovda eats you. (To death![2])

Another creepily human-like monster, known as the *chonchón*, comes to us from Peru. This fiend looks like a person, but at dusk, its head separates from its body and the chonchón starts flying around using its ears as wings. (They beat really fast, okay?) Then the chonchón swoops down and attacks people, biting them and sucking their blood. So it's a vampire with a detachable head. (Hmmm, that makes me wonder where its *stomach* is!)

And then there are the gross beasties that don't look human at all. Let's travel to the South Pacific, where a delicious

2.   Note: If you touch the ovda's left armpit, it will leave you alone. (This also works on some humans.)

monster called the *taua* can be found. According to the
legends of New Guinea, the taua is a fish that *looks* like it
would be good eating. But if you eat the taua, the taua will eat
you! The unfortunate person who makes a meal of this fish
will hear sinister laughter coming from inside him! That's
the taua, which has magically reassembled in the human's
stomach, and will begin chowing down in there immediately. (I guess a considerate human would then swallow
tartar sauce to help him taste better to his dinner guest!)

Since it lives in the neighborhood, let me tell you about my
favorite monster. Its name is the *sigbin*, and it comes from
the Philippines. At first, the sigbin doesn't seem all that
scary. It's about the size and shape of a medium-size dog.

THE SIGBIN ATTACKS!

But it has a number of interesting abilities. For example, it can suck blood from shadows, and it can also clap its ears together like hands. But what makes this creature special is its flatulence. The tiniest whiff of one of these monster farts is fatal. (Hey, just like my dog!)

And that brings me back to Japan again, because one of its most famous monsters is a water goblin called the *kappa*. If a human swimmer makes the kappa angry, the goblin will come up beneath the paddler and pull his intestines out through his—uh—poop chute.

Ouch! What might annoy the kappa enough to do this? Let's just say you should never pee while swimming.

As you can guess, the kappa is strongly associated with poop. After all, this monster is known for its horrible gas, as well as the fact that it has *three* anuses. Now that's *almost* as scary as a zombie eating a calzone!

EVERYONE POOPS

All hail the king!

Poop is the Dark Lord of All Things Gross. Yes, it's guaranteed to get a strong reaction from pretty much everyone. This has given poop a bad reputation, but we have to give it some credit for being a good teacher! After all, it taught you how to be disgusted. You see, there was once a day when you didn't care how many crickets or hairballs you stuck in your mouth. But at some point, a well-meaning adult (thanks, Mom!) started your potty-training program.

In addition to laying out the basics of where to sit (the toilet) and what to wipe with (no, not your socks!), you were taught NOT TO TOUCH YOUR POOP. Poop was off-limits! It was icky, gross, and to be avoided at all costs.

Of course, people have been training their kids this way for ages. For example, in medieval times, the people in Iceland built their outhouses far, far away from their homes—a symbol of how they felt about poop. And as recounted eight hundred years ago in the best-selling *Laxdœla Saga*, if you wanted to lay siege to a community in Iceland, you just surrounded it. You weren't trying to starve the residents

SADLY SICK SYNONYMS

butt paste	butt mud
devil's curry	voodoo butter
road apples	hazardous material
night soil	Lincoln logs
ordure	number two
stool	crapola

out—you were making them poop in their homes (which didn't have indoor plumbing!). This would ensure a quick surrender.

★ **LEEP:** To wash with cow dung and water. How much cow dung should you mix with the water? Just keep mixing it until it looks right. In other words, look before you leep!

THE ATTACK OF THE LIVING BUTT MUD

Okay, kids, gather around the campfire. Is everyone comfortable? No? Good! Now, there's nothing like a scary story told out in the woods, right?

Okay, okay, stop screaming! I won't get to the scary part for a bit. First, to understand this story, you need to know where poop comes from. No, not from the Poop Fairy.

It turns out that you digest food and make poop by flexing your muscles. What muscles? I'm talking about the digestive muscles deep inside your body.

POOPING? POP OFF!

Helpful phrases to say when you're ready to go "number two":

My colon just sent me an IM.

I've got to go bury a Quaker.

Captain, we have a message from the poop deck!

I'm going to go sit on the thunderbox.

Pilot to bombardier: Open main hatchway!

I've got to drop the kids off at the pool.

I have to bust a grumpy.

I've got to drop the Browns off at the Super Bowl.

I'm experiencing a peristaltic rush (*scientific!*).

I need to answer nature's call.

I'm prepared to unhitch a load.

I'm taking a poop/dump.[1]

1. But unless you are very strange, you do not ever really *take* a poop. You *leave* one!

Here's how it works. After you chew and swallow something, the chewed-up food starts heading to your food tube. On the way, your body starts closing trapdoors! That's because you don't want your food ending up in your lungs or up in your nose, do you?

Once the food finds the food tube ("esophagus"), gravity and a squeezing motion force it down to a valve that sits just above your stomach. That valve opens, and SPLASH! The chewed-up stuff lands in your stomach.

Now, your stomach is shaped sort of like the letter "J" with a big fat middle. Think of the top of the letter as your

ONE SMALL POOP FOR ME, ONE GIANT POOP FOR MANKIND

When *Apollo 11* astronaut Neil Armstrong landed on the moon in 1969, he left behind an American flag that is still there today. Armstrong also left behind his "Defecation Collection Devices." (That's right: there's astronaut poop on the moon!)

esophagus. Once it arrives, food might sit in your J—er, stomach—for up to four hours while it gets broken down by the acids that are pooled there. While the food breaks down (from the acid) and gets slimy (from stomach mucus), small contractions of the stomach push the food over to the side toward another valve, which leads to your small intestine.

COLOR COORDINATION

Once upon a time, there was a pirate captain who changed into a red shirt every time his ship engaged in battle. One day, one of his crew members asked the captain why he did this.

"It's so that if I'm cut or shot, I don't want my crew seeing the blood and thinking that all is lost!" the captain answered.

At that moment, the lookout cried from the crow's nest, "Captain, there are ten British warships headed this way!"

The captain whirled around and said to the curious crew member, "Fetch me my brown pants."

The small intestine should be called the long intestine, because it can be stretched out over thirty feet. Don't actually *do* that though, as it's usually coiled around inside you like a really long, hollow, big hot dog. (That's about how wide it is!) This is where most of the nutrients get sucked out of your food. Your pancreas, liver, and gallbladder all assist in this process by throwing in their own special chemicals.

Like your stomach, your small intestine is coated on the inside with mucus. This keeps it gooey and disgusting. *Sweet!* And it also helps keep your digested food (called "chyme") moving. But digested food doesn't move very fast; sometimes it only goes about an inch a minute. So it can take up to five hours to move through the small intestine.

WARNING:

If you don't have enough water in your body, your intestines AND your poop can dry out. If you've ever been constipated, you know that your poop can turn into a hard clay. And that hard clay moves slowly inside you, while it gets more and more compacted. And when it's time for it to come out, you might be making a face like this:

POP QUIZ!

If you were a king or a queen, would you wear your crown in the bathroom? (Don't worry, there is no wrong answer.)

Unless you said "yes." (That's the wrong answer!)

To fix this problem, lay off the junk food, drink LOTS of water, and eat some fruit. And good luck to you.

And now, on to the large intestine!

Also called the colon, the large intestine is wider than the small intestine, but at three to five feet in length, it's much shorter. The large intestine looks like a big "n." It connects to your small intestine on the right side of your body, goes up over the small intestine, and then heads down the left side of your body. Finally, it takes a turn and centers inside the middle of your butt. (More on that later!)

The digested food that hits the large intestine needs another three to ten hours of digestion to finally become "poop." As the stuff works its way through the large intestine, the last nutrients are pulled out of it. The large intestine also removes most of the water from this neo-poop. This means that as your poop travels, it gets drier and harder. When everything is said and done, only about 35 percent of the food you eat will come back out again.

As your poop heads to the exit (aka, the anal sphincter), it gets molded into the individual logs that you see in the toilet. These logs finally hit the last eight inches of your large intestine, a magical section known as the RECTUM. As your rectum fills with poop, you'll start getting that special feeling that could be summed up as: "I gots to go!"

Your anal sphincter is what holds back your poop from dropping into your shorts. Do you know how important this is? Think about how many times it has saved you from hideous embarrassment. So let's have three cheers for the anal sphincter!

And now we come to the scary part of the story. See how I'm shining my flashlight on something big and brown at the edge of the forest over there? Well, you should be scared, because now I'm going to tell you about ...

THE ATTACK OF THE LIVING BUTT MUD!

Your poop is ALIVE! Yep, up to 30 percent of your Lincoln logs are composed of bacteria. Even a tiny dab of

THEY COOLED OFF

In 1971, a band named Hot Poop released a record titled *Does Their Own Stuff!* They were never heard from again.

it might have trillions of those little poopers. Some of the bacteria are dead (they don't live very long), but plenty of those little organisms are still eating away at the mucus and indigestible stuff like vegetable and grain fibers. Bacteria is what makes your poop smell like . . . poop. The more bacteria in your poop, the more it stinks!

FOOD AND POOP: THE INSIDE SCOOP

The average total weight of a poop is about half a pound.

If you eat a lot of fatty foods, your poop will float! (This is not a good enough reason to eat fatty foods.)

If you eat a lot of meat, your poop will reek!

If you eat a lot of cheese and other dairy products, your poop will stink less than other people's.

A BOWEL MOVEMENT IS A MANY-SPLENDORED THING

Members of a tribe in the Amazon basin are willing to eat almost anything. So maybe it's no coincidence that their language has a hundred different words for diarrhea!

By the way, although you should always avoid other people's poop, you don't really have anything to worry about from your own butt mud. You see, it's difficult to get a disease from your own poop that you don't have already! Oh, and I should tell you that another thing in your poop's mix is "bile" from your gallbladder. Bile helps break down fats. It starts off as yellow or green, but by the time you see your poop, it will be a nice brown or maybe a brownish-green color.

THE WORLD'S GREATEST HEADLINE

A journalist in Sydney, Australia, wrote an article about police officers issuing tickets to smokers caught dumping their cigarette butts in the street. The story's headline: "May the Butt Force Be with You."

AND NOW, THE REAL HORROR: DIARRHEA!

As you know, your large intestine removes water from the food you're digesting. But what if there's something wrong with that food? Maybe it's way too spicy (chili peppers, anyone?) or your body realizes it has harmful toxins in it. Travelers frequently get diarrhea because they are continually exposed to food (accompanied by germs and bacteria) that they don't ordinarily eat. That's why there are names for it like "Montezuma's revenge," the "Aztec two-step," and "Delhi belly."

As your body realizes it's in distress, an alarm goes off all the way from your stomach to your colon. Your digestive system decides that the food needs to be removed from the body as quickly as possible. And so the semi-digested food is rushed through your digestive system: "Show those bums the door!" In the large intestine, where water is usually taken from the food, your body will instead actually *add* water to it. This makes the toxic poop get through your guts that much faster!

The end of the story isn't pretty. You rush to the toilet and spew diarrhea. (Sorry, I couldn't think of a nice way to say it.) While this is not a pleasant experience, remember that your body is just doing its job!

YOU'RE ALWAYS PACKIN' HEAT

At any given time, your large intestine contains poop, even if you just went to the bathroom.

The only way to get *all* of that poop out is with an enema! If you don't know what an enema is, ask your science teacher or your grandparents. Or just read the following:

Getting an enema involves sticking a tube into the anus. This tube is attached to a container or bladder filled with water. Then water is squirted through the tube and into the rectum. As the large intestine fills with water, the person feels pretty weird.

Why would a person go through this torture? Enemas clean out the large intestine. And they can help with really bad constipation. So even though it sounds ridiculous, some people who aren't being held at gunpoint have been known to voluntarily get enemas.

Life is crazy!

REMOTE-CONTROL ENEMA

A Japanese company sells a high-tech bidet (bih-DAY) that will spray and clean your backside. It even has a remote control to use for an enema wash! According to the company, "The warm water stream passes directly through the rectum and fills the lower colon for a more thorough cleansing and expelling of feces and gas."

CHART YOUR SUCCESS!

Doctors have come up with a simple way of measuring how long it takes poop to go through a patient. Specifically, by looking at the shape and form of a poop, they can tell how long it's been in the patient's colon. This "transit time" helps the doctors make judgments about the patient's health.

Little Coconuts
See the lumpies? It's hard to bust those grumpies!
Ease of Pooping: Very difficult

The Baby Ruth
A candy bar chock-full of nuts never looked so bad.
Ease of Pooping: Can be difficult

The Voodoo Pickle
Some say this is the perfect poop!
Ease of Pooping: Pretty good

The Snake
Voted most likely to circle into a tidy coil.
Ease of Pooping: Just right?

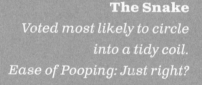

Shotgun Blast
Soft pellets.
Ease of Pooping: Easy

Mango Express
First you're dashing, then you're splashing.
Ease of Pooping: Too Easy

The Dreaded Gombu
Since this is pure liquid, splashing is a major drawback.
Ease of Pooping: Good grief, what happened?

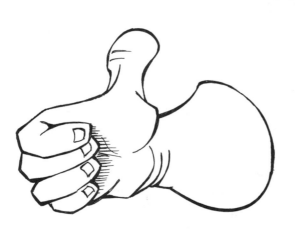

A person suffering from *really* bad constipation can suffer from what's known as "fecal impaction." Translation: The poop in the rectum has hardened into plaster. No amount of fluid, fruit, or enemas can fix this. In order to get things moving again, a doctor has to actually go in and physically break up the hard poop in the colon. (If you've ever had to use a coat hanger to break up the poop in a clogged toilet pipe, you get the idea.)

So remember to avoid all forms of constipation by eating lots of bran, vegetables, and fruit!

Now we can all sit back and relax—oh, rats, I thought I was done with the back door's gross stuff. But I forgot to mention that there are a lot of veins in the region of your poop chute. Sometimes these veins can get enlarged and swollen. This hurts, and it's also pretty horrible to see because the veins can get pretty big. This condition is called hemorrhoids. That's a nasty name for an unfortunate condition.

WHO WILL SIT ON THE STOOL OF POWER?

Are you interested in the sport of competitive pooping? To play, you need to have at least one opponent who isn't shy about showing the results of his or her bowel movements. There are an infinite number of ways to play! Here are just a couple:

1. ENVIRONMENTAL GLADIATORS: Who can use the *least* amount of toilet paper? Not only does this save trees, but it also gives your wastewater plant a lighter load. In terms of strategy, keep in mind that the more solid a poop is, the easier it is to wipe.

Caution: Don't wipe less just to win. Nothing is worse than walking around with "dew on your lily," "dingleberries," or "butt lint."

2. BATTER UP! Using the chart on page 105, agree on a scoring system like baseball for your poops. A reasonably healthy and sizable poop could be judged as a single or double. A really impressive poop that requires little or no wiping could be a triple. And one that breaks the surface of the toilet water could be a home run!

OTHER CATEGORIES:

LITTLE SQUIRT = FOUL BALL

MEAGER PELLETS = BUNT

PERSON HAS AN "AT BAT" AND CAN'T PRODUCE = INNING OVER!

CLOGGED TOILET = GAME CALLED ON ACCOUNT OF RAIN

Note: You may need to enlist an umpire who is willing to impartially score your poops. (I'm sure there are all sorts of people who would like to do this.)

PUBLIC SERVICE ANNOUNCEMENT

The time will come when you have to poop really bad and there's no toilet in sight. We've all been through this torture, and it's horrible. But there is, apparently, a solution to it. No, don't poop your pants! What's wrong with you?

A Korean scientist came up with something called the "Su-jok therapy." I am not making this up. When you feel the need to bury a Quaker, get a pen or pencil (or something similar) and trace a circle clockwise on your left palm, or counterclockwise on your right. I'll admit that I haven't had a chance to try this yet, but a trusted source tells me it works!

BATHROOM READING

When reading the classics of literature (like this book!), many people are shocked by the language they find. For example, Geoffrey Chaucer's *The Canterbury Tales*, written in the 1300s, is required reading for today's English scholars. One of the tales features a character who says, "You would make me kiss the seat of your old pants and swear it was the relic of a saint, even though it was smeared by your—"[2]

2. I updated the language. The original reads, "Thou woldest make me kisse thyn olde breech and swere it were a relyk of a seint, though it were with thy fundement depeint!"

ANTISOCIAL POOPERS

When visiting the zoo, you may have noticed that some of the primates may throw poop at the human spectators. Can you blame them? If I got thrown behind bars and had to stay on a place called "Monkey Island," I'd probably practice my fastball with a few grumpies myself!

Humans can be even worse than primates when they get mad. For example, in 1995, a bank executive named Gerard Finneran pitched a fit onboard an international flight. Angry that no one would serve him more alcohol, Finneran climbed aboard the drink cart, pooped on it, and then walked around the aircraft smearing his feces in the aisles.

At his court appearance, Finneran told the judge, "I promise you will never hear of me doing anything like this again." Gee, what a relief!

Punishing poopy wrongdoers reminds me of a story called *The Divine Comedy*, written by Italian poet Dante Alighieri in the early 1300s. In his story, Dante is given a tour of both hell and paradise. While visiting hell, Dante notices that there is poop in the river Styx! (Raw sewage in the nether-world?) Dante also sees that people who were suck-ups and flatterers during their lives have to basically roll around in poop in the afterlife.

I guess Dante didn't like brown-nosers!

PHILOSOPHY AND POOP

Famous Greek philosopher Heraclitus (540–480 BCE) suffered from a medical condition called edema. He apparently thought that a lot of cow manure could solve his problem. So he had a *lot* of wet, steaming cow manure gathered together. Then he immersed his body in the cow manure. Then he drowned in the cow manure.

Fascinating!

Finally, let's end this section with the poetry of Chinese philosopher Zhuangzi. Over two thousand years ago, he wrote:

*TILL NOW I THOUGHT
THAT DEATH BEFELL
THE UNTALENTED ALONE.
IF THOSE WITH TALENT, TOO,
MUST DIE
SURELY THEY MAKE
BETTER MANURE.*

POOP IN THE ANIMAL KINGDOM

Hey, did you know there's a company that makes paper out of the poop of Australian marsupials like wombats and kangaroos? The company is on the island-state of Tasmania, and the kangaroo poop paper is called "Roo-Poo"!

You can probably guess the problem the company had with the envelopes they made. That's right, nobody wanted to lick them! For research, I decided to see what kangaroo poo looks like, and it's pretty much the way I'd imagined it: *poo-ey*. But it made me wonder: What animal has the biggest poop on the planet?

But then I thought, "That's dumb. Isn't there more to life than wondering what animal makes the most colossal caca?"

Of course there is!

I'll think of something in a second.

All right, nothing better comes to mind, so we'd better look into this! When it comes to the size of their grumpies, big animals don't necessarily make big poops. For example, a full-grown moose can weigh a thousand pounds, but its droppings might be an inch long. Heck, there are wombats that poop bigger than that!

When a whale poops, a lot does come out. But between the poop coming out underwater and being rather liquidy to

LIQUID GOLD

Sperm whales eat squid. Lots of squid. But as anyone who's seen *20,000 Leagues Under the Sea* knows, squids have sharp pointy beaks. These are hard to digest, and so sperm whales have a special fatty mucus in their intestines that safely coats the beaks in a gooey mess.

After the sperm whale poops out the mucus/squid beak mess, it's called "ambergris." This has a unique smell that perfume-makers love to use in expensive products like Chanel No. 5. How rare is ambergris? Let's just say that you can get over $4,000 for a pound of the stuff!

start with, there's no good way to judge the size of a whale's poop pile.

As for elephants, they can *really* deliver the goods. But the biggest poop pile I've seen is from a rhinoceros. (Just imagine an average-size horse poop and then multiply by ten and you'll get an idea of what I mean.) But I guess if we're going to talk big poop, maybe we should start with the dinosaurs!

Scientists are constantly analyzing the fossils of animals from millions of years ago. This goes for their poop, too! The word we use for fossilized poops is *coprolites*, or "dung-stones."

These poops are obviously pretty old, in that they have turned into ROCKS with no organic matter left in them. Even so, scientists have noticed that anyone who sees a coprolite will try to smell it!

Coprolites are rare—or maybe just really hard to recognize! That's because poop is soft, and it's likely to be stepped on, rained on, and squished before turning into a fossil. The largest stone-poop from a meat-eating dinosaur is currently a seventeen-inch-long turd that probably came from a *Tyrannosaurus Rex*.

That's some serious poop!

Paleoscatologist Karen Chin has found the poops of a duck-billed dinosaur called *Maiasaura*. Poops from this dinosaur usually look sort of like really gigantic cow patties.

★ **PALEOSCATOLOGIST:** A scientist who specializes in fossilized poop.

SHREW POOP IS GOOD FOOD

The tiniest mammal in the world is the shrew. Although its poop is not very impressive, the Borneo tree shrew uses an organic toilet.

You might have seen pictures of pitcher plants before. These are tropical plants that grow pitcher-shaped pouches filled with a bug-attracting liquid. After the bugs are trapped in this juice, the pitcher plant absorbs nutrients from the insects. But in Borneo, the pitcher plant works a little differently. Tree shrews come and eat sap from the top of the plant's pitcher. Since the shrew's butt is often situated right over the pouch, the small mammal then poops down into it. (What's weird is that the pitcher even looks like a toilet.) And the pitcher plant then processes and feeds on the shrew poop!

SECOND TIME'S A CHARM

Beavers eat tree bark. And after a beaver eats bark, it poops out an oatmeal-looking pile of partially digested bark. Then the beaver eats its poop. After the beaver digests it a second time, the poop comes out looking like sawdust.

It's not just paleoscatologists who save reptile poop. Daniel Bennett is a herpetologist, or expert on reptiles. And as a PhD student, Bennett traveled to the Philippines to gather samples of the rare Butaan lizard. In the process, he became a lizard poop expert! "By the beginning of the third year of my PhD, I knew more about lizard feces than I had ever thought possible," he said. For five long years, he gathered his data. But, one day, when he was out doing fieldwork, someone threw away his entire lizard-poop collection!

That must have been a sad day.

POOP EATERS

Dung beetles eat poop. "What's a dung beetle?" you ask? Aren't you paying attention? It's a beetle that eats poop!

★ **COPROPHAGY:** Eating poop.

A dung beetle's whole life has to do with poop. For example, its mating ritual literally revolves around poop. Working together, a male and female dung beetle roll some poop into a ball. And it's true love.

Dung beetles eat all sorts of dung: elephant dung, camel dung, sheep dung, you name it. But most dung beetles prefer horse dung. Now you know.

Similar to the dung beetle is the scarab beetle. When it finds a nice steaming pile of dung, it sorts through it, gathering and rolling only the purest and tastiest parts of the poop. Once the dung ball is about the size of your fist, the beetle starts rolling it away from the original poop pile so that it can eat it in peace. ("Roll, roll, roll the poop ...") But, of course, the dung ball is way bigger than the beetle, so this can take a while.

In the privacy of the poop, male and female scarab beetles can lay eggs. Then their larvae can safely grow up in the poop. And if they get hungry, the larvae can just take a bite out of their nursery!

POOP HAPPENS ... TO BE A GOOD PLACE TO LIVE

Amphibians need to keep moist in order to survive. And that's why small toads in Sri Lanka bury themselves inside piles of elephant poop during the hot, dry part of the year!

It's a Gross Job, But I Don't Want to Do It!

There are a lot of gross jobs in the world. And I had the worst one of all.

In high school, I was a cook at a well-known fried-chicken chain. And one of my jobs included the four most feared words in the English language:

Cleaning the grease traps.

This job is pretty much what it sounds like. All day long, the chickens were cooked in boiling grease, and as they bubbled in their oily lava, bits of chicken skin, fat, and breading fell to the bottom of the cooker. That was the grease trap.

Toward the end of the day, the grease trap was opened. Kneeling under the pressure cooker, I got to enjoy the sight of brown molten grease mixed with cooked chicken bits pouring out of it. The whole concoction looked like diarrhea spewing out of a robot. (Oh, sorry about that!)

Although it was pretty bad, I wonder how "grease-trap cleaner" stacks up against some of the other horrible jobs throughout history:

ROYAL BUTT WIPER: In medieval kingdoms, the king was deemed too important to wipe his own butt. So someone else did it for him. And since toilet paper wasn't invented until centuries later, it was important for a butt wiper to have soft hands and a gentle touch.

GARBAGEOLOGIST: This person studies garbage. Next!

LEECH COLLECTOR: How do you collect leeches? You walk through swamps full of leeches. Then you pick them off your body to start your collection.

SPITBOY: A human-powered rotisserie! If an entire animal was impaled on a stake (known as a "spit") and put over a fire, it needed to be turned. The spitboy took care of the turning!

RAT CATCHER: During the Age of Exploration, many sailing ships had full-time rat catchers onboard. The longer the ship was at sea, the nicer the crew was to the rat catcher. (The fresh rat meat was highly prized!)

FORENSIC ENTOMOLOGIST: Police detectives who are also insect specialists solve murders by investigating the insects found on dead bodies. And the bugs get to help. (Corpse maggots and cheese skippers can put criminals behind bars?)

HAZARDOUS MATERIALS DIVER: As you know, one in five people pees in the pool. So the next time you're taking a dip, remember to put on a diving suit that completely covers your body! It's helpful if you have to swim through any sewage. (You know, like if your cousin tries to force some gas out and makes a poopy mistake? "Toxic spill!")

Hmmm, maybe cleaning the grease traps wasn't so bad after all. Let's see, what other bad jobs are out there?

Actually, you've done some of them yourself. After all, housework is *really* gross. For example, dust mites are flying all over the place when you vacuum! Heck, dust mites live *inside* the vacuum. The only thing that outnumbers dust mites in your house are dust mite corpses and dust mite poops. What are these horrible creatures eating? You! (Your dead skin, that is.)

As for working in the kitchen, forget about it. The kitchen sponge might be one of the most revolting things in your whole house. It's swarming with bacteria. When you wipe down a counter, you're smearing bacteria all over the place!

THE BACTERIA BUNCH

Okay, but everyone has to do housework. What about more specialized jobs, like ones where people work alongside flesh-eating beetles? The good people at Skulls Unlimited International can tell you all about this. Skulls Unlimited is a company where people clean and polish skulls and other bones from a variety of animals. (Including humans!)

THIS JOB SUCKS!

Do you think it would be better to clean up after living people or dead ones? Dunno! But I do know that I don't like to vacuum the house. I mention this because plastic surgeons vacuum fat from living people. That sucks slightly more than vacuuming the carpet.

But how do you get a nice tidy skull from a messy decapitated head? The process begins with the removal of the head's tissues ... by hand. *Blech!* But how do you get all the little pieces of meat off? By putting a bunch of flesh-eating beetles on the skull to eat the leftovers!

Is this nasty? Well, the owner of Skulls Unlimited is Jay Villemarette, and he said, "It *is* nasty." So there you have it! But my favorite quote came from one of his employees about what's *really* gross: "I've been waist-deep in a dead hippopotamus, and I'd rather do that than change diapers."

But just as there's supposedly more than one way to skin a cat, there are also apparently at least two ways to clean skulls. For a second option, let's visit the people who lived on the Torres Strait Islands near Australia. The tradition in their culture was to cut off the heads of their dead. The

WHEN YOU MAKE A MESS AND CAN'T CLEAN IT UP YOURSELF

After a murder, who cleans up the crime scene? Not the police; when their investigation is done, they're out of there. So there are a number of businesses specializing in cleaning up after crime scenes. They often call themselves "decontamination" services.

Most of these companies will take care of grisly homicide, suicide, and car accident scenes. It's an odd business. I mean, there aren't many repeat customers! And as one decontamination expert explains, it's hard to advertise. "It's not like I can put out a 2-for-1 coupon," she says.

heads were then put on top of ant colonies. Between the heat and the ants, it was only a matter of time before there was just a skull there. The skull was then painted red and used for decoration. (Decoration?!)

SOMEDAY I MIGHT BE AN ACTOR!

Here's a story of a really tough job. But first, you need to know that Shakespeare's play *Hamlet* has a scene with the skull of a dead man named Yorick.

Okay, now stick with me: Del Close was a Chicago actor/ comedian. Shortly before his death in 1999, Close made his friend Charna Halpern promise to donate his skull to a local theater. That way, Close could play the part of Yorick even though he was dead. See what a hard worker he was? He wanted to stay on the job even after death!

Halpern agreed. But when she asked the people at the hospital if they would cut off Close's head after he died, they just laughed. And as hard as she looked, Halpern couldn't find anyone to cut off Close's head! Eventually, Close was cremated with his head still attached.

So Halpern decided to get a "stand-in skull" from an anatomy shop. She found one that looked right, and then she took it home to pull the skull's teeth out. She did this because Close had worn dentures! But it was another tough job. As Halpern said, "Pulling teeth is like pulling teeth." (Everyone's a comedian!)

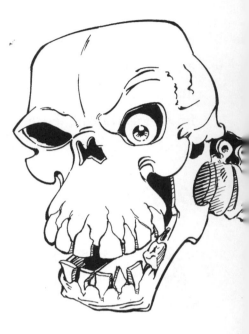

Anyway, then Halpern donated the fake "Del Close skull" to a Chicago theater. It was the most famous skull in the city! Years passed, and then a reporter at the *Chicago Tribune* investigated the story. Halpern confessed to what she had done. (Hey, I don't blame her; she tried to do the right thing. But take it from me, cutting off your best friend's head isn't easy.)

SHRINKING HEADS

All this talk of decapitation has got me wondering about shrunken heads. These are the actual heads of humans that are small enough to attach to a key ring. But who gets to make them? Is it a hard job? And how did the skulls get so shrimpy?

The answers to these questions come from high in the Andes, where the people of the Jivaros tribe are famed headshrinkers. The Jivaros live in what is now Ecuador and Peru. And back in the day, if you were a member of their tribe and went to battle, you might get lucky and kill somebody. Then you would return home with the head of one of your enemies. Then you'd do the following:

1 Chop off the head of your enemy. (You already did that, right?)

2 Make a vertical cut down the back of the head and neck and carefully peel the flesh off the skull. (The decapitated person is now "losing face.")

3 Sew the eyes and mouth shut.

4 Put some small stones around the base of a fire. Hang a pot of water over it. Now boil the head skin for two hours. During this time, you'll notice that it's sort of like a wool sweater in the dryer: it shrinks!

5 Pull the head skin out of the water and fill it with some of the hot rocks that you put around the fire. As the rocks cool, replace them with hot sand. Keep replacing the sand until the skin is "cured" and looks smooth from the outside. When you think the curing is done, sew up the slit in the back of the head as you go, so that the sand filling will stay put.

6 Now hang the head by its hair over a smoky fire for five to eight hours. This will dry it out, shrink it some more, and give the head the shiny, leathery look you're looking for. The shrunken head should be about the size of your fist!

7 Attach the shrunken head to a keychain. Sell it to American tourists.

RUMPOLOGY!

Humans have come up with a wide variety of ways to tell the future. And one of the strangest of these is rumpology, or the "art" of looking at (or feeling!) a person's butt and then reading his or her fate from it.

For the record, I am not making any of this up.

What can a butt tell us? A lot of things, I guess, but none of them very good! I'd say that if you can predict someone's future from looking at his or her butt, their future must be pretty bleak.

The most famous rumpologist is Sylvester Stallone's mother, Jacqueline. She encourages people to take a photo of their butt and send it in with $125 to get a butt reading. How hard could it be? As she says, your butt print "will reveal your whole being."

You know, now that I think about it, I am sort of curious to know what my butt has to say about me. Would it talk trash? Maybe my butt holds the secrets of the universe? (Now I have to see if there's a good rumpologist in my area   .)

TOILETS!

Toilets make life wonderful!

After all, think about what you would have done *today* without a toilet. My guess is that you'd be having a terrible, horrible, no good, very bad day.

But inventing a toilet that flushes turned out to be a pretty hard thing to do. The first flushing toilet dates back to ancient Greece. But it was far too elaborate and expensive to make, so only royal bottoms got to sit on it. It would be thousands of years before Sir John Harrington (1561–1612), a member of Queen Elizabeth's royal court, invented the first flushing and refilling toilet with moving parts. And even it had the same problem that *all* toilets had: STINK. You see, sewer gas would float up the pipes and make the entire bathroom stink like . . . a sewer!

Stopping sewer gas is one of the great achievements of mankind! If you look under your toilet today, you'll see that the drainage pipe bends away in an S-shaped curve. There is always some water in the bottom of the curve, and that's what stops sewer smells from stinking up the room you're in. This great idea came about thanks to Sir Thomas Crapper (1836–1910) and other Victorian Age plumbers.

Thanks, Crapper!

POTTY MOUTHS

Over the course of time, the French have not gotten on very well with the English. So the French called bathrooms *lieux à langlaise*: "English places."

That's mean!

The French language has made nicer contributions to the world, though. For example, by the 1800s, the French word *toilette* (which literally means "cloth") had come to mean a room or place where washing and dressing takes place. Eventually, "toilet" was used to refer only to the convenient indoor plumbing device you pee and poop into. If you go to Japan, odds are they'll call it a *toiretto*. (Really!)

Back in the good old days, Europeans spent the night filling up bedpans and thunder mugs. In the morning, they'd often empty these poop and pee containers right out the window. But since dumping bodily liquids on someone's head is pretty uncool, the French got in the habit of shouting *"Guardez l'eau!"* ("Look out for this water!") before flinging fluids. This was eventually shortened to simply crying *"L'eau!"*

And that's how one of the words for bathroom came about: loo.[1] (It's also why streets in the old days really reeked.)

1. Medieval monks called the loo the "necessary house." Other names rooted in history include water closet, privy, lavatory, and House of Easement.

Today, nobody—I mean *nobody*— can beat the Japanese for high-tech toilets. Japanese scientists have made the toilet a household throne with a wide array of interesting accessories and features, including heated seats, interior lighting, and music consoles. There is also a feature that lets the toilet know whether or not you want a tiny electrical charge to be sent through your buttocks to check on your body fat ratio. One brand of Japanese toilet even remembers exactly what temperature you want the seat to be set at. It also has a retractable spray nozzle that will shoot a comfortable and cleansing jet of water at your, uh, well, you know. And the latest robo-toilets can tell the gender of users and then automatically lift or lower the toilet seat accordingly.

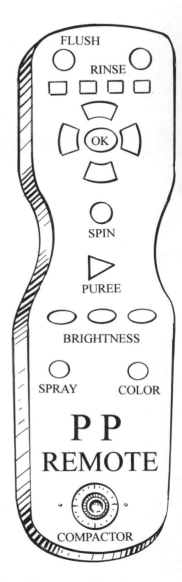

BOY (*outraged*): Hey, why does the toilet automatically lower its lid when I come in the bathroom?

GIRL (*laughing*): Someone must have programmed it to think you're a girl!

I'M GOING TO GO WATCH THE TOILET

The Fish 'n' Flush allows you to replace your regular toilet tank with a new one that has an aquarium around it. So when you walk into the bathroom, you see an aquarium behind the toilet seat! A marine biologist helped design it so that the fish aren't affected when the toilet is flushed.

This is amazing, because before World War II, almost all Japanese squatted over pits to relieve themselves! But rebuilding the country after war allowed Japan to modernize the whole country incredibly fast. That meant all of the Japanese who were used to hunkering down over a hole had to get used to sitting on a toilet. And while it might not seem like it to you, this change was a BIG deal. Writer Yoko Mure shared that the new style seemed the same as "sitting on a chair. I had a terror that if I got used to it, I might excrete whenever I was sitting on a chair anywhere, even at a lesson or at mealtimes."

Other countries have faced similar problems when making the change to modern plumbing. The Southeast

Asian country of Malaysia has started replacing cesspits (where poopers squat over a hole in the ground) with flushing toilets. But lots of Malaysians still squat—while standing on the toilet seat!

FANCY MEETING YOU HERE!

Many public bathrooms in China are "open-style," so when a squatting visitor looks up, he or she might be face-to-face with another person squatting over another pit.

TO WIPE OR NOT TO WIPE: THAT IS THE QUESTION

In addition to pee and poo, there's one other thing that constantly gets flushed. Know what it is? That's right, toilet paper. But did you know there are billions of people who don't use toilet paper at all? That's because when it comes to "getting the dew off the lily," you can go dry (with TP) or wet (with H_2O).

I'm betting that you're a wiper, not a washer, so I should probably explain the idea of a bidet (bih-DAY). First invented in the late Middle Ages, this bathroom fixture is usually placed next to the toilet. The idea is that after you poop, a geyser of warm water is better at cleaning your butt than a wad of dry paper.

Here's how it works. After pooping, the person straddles the bidet, which often looks like a small porcelain bowl. The user then either sits on the bidet or squats over it, depending on whether the bidet has jets of water shooting sideways across its bowl or if it has a little fountain that burbles up. A bidet also usually has a knob to adjust water temperature and a lever to adjust water pressure. Then, after washing the dew off his or her lily, the user dries off with some toilet paper. *Ta-dah!*

IF THIS SOUNDS WEIRD TO YOU, THINK OF IT THIS WAY: IF YOUR WHOLE BODY WERE COVERED IN POOP, HOW WOULD YOU WANT TO CLEAN OFF?

a. By wiping your body off with dry paper.

b. By washing with clean water.

See what I mean? Writer Dave Praeger thinks the reason bidets haven't caught

TAKE THAT, SUPER-VILLAIN!

An American company printed Adolf Hitler's face on toilet paper during World War II.

135

WIPING RULES TO LIVE BY

After a perfect poop, you don't need to wipe at all—but do it anyway, just to be sure!

After a normal poop, you may have to wipe two to five times.

If you have to wipe more than six to ten times, you pretty much need to take a shower to take care of business. (Or wash off in the buttsink!)

Ultra-soft, quilted toilet paper can't be made from recycled paper. So consider using regular ply!

on everywhere is because they sound too . . . French. He thinks they'd be much more popular if they were called "buttsinks." But bidets *are* common in Europe and Japan.

There's no question that people who live in "wiping" cultures end up with dirty underwear. Can you say "bacon strips"? One scientist marveled that wipers complain about a soup stain on a tablecloth while "sitting in their fecally stained pants." That's nasty! And that's also why the word "dingleberry" is used to describe the dried poop attached to the hair around the anus. (A cranberry that grows in the

MMMM, BACON STRIPS!

southeastern United States is also called a dingleberry. Just to be safe, don't eat any!)

Which method has been around longer—washing or wiping—is hard to say. Toilet paper on a roll wasn't available until the 1880s. And since it cost the modern equivalent of over $10 per roll, it wasn't very popular! So what were people wiping with before that? Well, there were the usual suspects, like moss, grass, straw, and leaves. In the Middle East, people might wipe with small stones, followed by a water cleanup. The ancient Romans used a short stick with a sponge attached to the end of it. The

THIS BOOK STINKS!

When Roman poet Gaius Catullus (about 84 BCE–54 CE) read something he didn't like, he called it *cacata charta*— "poop paper."

137

THE HORROR!

Most cultures have branded the bathroom as a place to be avoided. But Japan is one of the few places where it's also been associated with monsters! Many Japanese children are led to believe that a hairy hand might emerge from the toilet and grab them! Add to this the fact that, historically, bathrooms in Japan were hidden away in a dark part of the house, and you have a recipe for toilet terror!

sponge was soaked in saltwater (or rose water!) and then scrubbed around. This excellent method degraded in the Middle Ages to "gompf" sticks, which were designed to scrape. (But even a gompf stick was probably better than the corncobs used by American settlers.)

The Vikings wiped with handfuls of wool, which sounds perfectly reasonable, and on some South Pacific islands, coconut shells served their duty. During the Renaissance, French nobles picked up style points by using fancy lace napkins. And believe it or not, some cold weather cultures in North America and Siberia wiped with snow.

Whether washing or wiping, people generally use their left hand to get the dew off the lily. That's one reason why the left hand has picked up sort of a bad reputation! (In Italian, the word *sinistra* means both "left" and "sinister"!) And that's why it's VERY impolite in many cultures to eat or offer to shake with the left hand.

I always assumed that everyone wiped in the same direction: back to front. Nope! Lots of guys and most women wipe from front to back. But as far as I know, nobody wipes right to left, so that's a relief.

Also, I thought that all wipers did a "visual" on their paper to know when they're done. I've since learned that many people just wipe until they *think* they're clean. That's because they're too scared to look at their own toilet paper.

Now *that's* pretty squeamish!

HUMANURE

There are lots of organic and chemical fertilizers that people add to the soil to make it better for farming. And poop (or "manure") is one of the best fertilizers around! It's been used ever since the first human looked at a Brussels sprout and said, "I wonder if *I* could grow one of these. And where IS Brussels, anyway?"

Using farm-animal poop for manure makes sense, but if poop is good for crops, why not use human poop as well? After all, your poop is full of potassium, nitrogen, and phosphorus. (Your pee has the same stuff at about 80 percent of poop's strength.) And in the right amounts, these chemicals are great for fertilizer. So if a human makes manure, can you guess what we call it? *Humanure!* In Sweden, they have developed special toilets to treat humanure. These toilets separate the poop from the pee. ("Number 1, say goodbye to Number 2!") Treating the pee separately not only makes better manure, but it also produces methane (surprise!), which can be used as an energy source.

When human poop is processed properly, it looks like rich, brown-black dirt. It doesn't stink and it's not full of scary bacteria. In fact, if your family already composts, it looks just like what your leaves, food scraps, and lawn clippings turn into. And the heat that builds up in a compost pile will eventually kill any harmful bacteria that are hanging around.

And don't worry about the worms. A New Zealand man named Coll Bell invented a composting toilet that worked great. However, a government official wanted to know if the worms in the compost would be overworked or "traumatized" by having to dig in the poop. Mr. Bell then had to get a worm expert (known as a "vermiculturist") to assure the official that composting worms are "happy" worms!

So why aren't composting toilets being used all over the world? Because to use the ones that separate pee from poo, men have to pee sitting down. And in many countries (especially in North and South America), this is not seen as very manly. In fact, the German slang word *sitzpinkler* means both "man who sits to pee" and "wimp"! So if you have ever wondered if men who are worried about looking macho are slowing civilization down, you're on to something.

But wait, the *simplest* toilet might be the best one. A man named Joseph Jenkins (author of *The Humanure Handbook*) came up with this system. First, he builds a simple cabinet that's about as tall as a toilet seat. The cabinet has a big hole in the top, into which slides a five-gallon bucket. A regular toilet seat covers the hole when the bucket isn't in use. Next to the cabinet is a second bucket full of sawdust, with a scoop in it.

When a person needs to poop, he scoops some sawdust into the bucket in the cabinet. Then he sits and poops (and probably pees) on the sawdust. Finally, he scoops some sawdust over the poop and pee. That's it! The bucket will not smell. After about a week, the bucket is lifted out and emptied onto a compost heap, where it's covered with hay or straw. That compost pile will sit for a couple of years, and the poop really WILL be compost by the end of that time.

Then it can be used as manure in gardening! (Apparently, Jenkins grows prize-winning tomatoes with his home-grown compost.)

WORLD TOILET DAY ROCKS!

If all this potty talk has made you think we're living in the Golden Age of Toilets, that's only partly true. I mean, sure, *you're* lucky. If you needed to go to the bathroom right now, you probably could. High-five! (Uh, you washed your hands, right?)

But imagine if you were one of the 40 percent of the people in the world who don't have access to a toilet, outhouse, or even an empty coffee can. Billions of folks have to poop and/or pee in fields, forests, bushes, rivers, or open spaces. The result is what we call "open sewage," and it isn't just gross, it's bad for everyone's health. If you step on a pile of human poop, here's what can be found in a small portion of what's stuck to your sole:

10 MILLION VIRUSES

1 MILLION BACTERIA

100 WORM EGGS

1,000 PARASITES

1 PIECE OF BUBBLEGUM (HEY! THAT WAS ALREADY THERE!)

Yeesh! Open sewage is a particular problem in many poor, overpopulated countries. To look into the world's "toilet situation," a group of experts discovered some of the toughest places in the world to track down a decent bathroom. The African country of Eritrea was judged the worst place to be if you need to go. About 85 percent of Eritreans are forced to relieve themselves in the open because there are almost no toilets to be found.

But for school kids, the worst place to be if you need to go might be the country of Yemen. There, children often find themselves in schools without any restrooms. To cope, Yemeni students develop bladders of steel and hold it all day long. That would make it a little hard to concentrate on classwork! (The Yemeni boys usually end up peeing on their schools' walls. Really!)

The point is that the toilet (and the plumbing it's hooked up to) could be the greatest invention of all time. Don't believe me? Getting poop and its related germs out of your surroundings adds an average of twenty years to your lifespan!

(Want to know how many hours a television adds to your life? [2])

More than two million people die each year because of health problems related to open sewage. That's why a world health organization came up with the following poem to publicize the dangers of poop germs getting into drinking water:

JACK AND JILL WENT UP THE HILL
TO FETCH A PAIL OF WATER
AFTER A DRINK OF THE WATER
JACK DIED OF CHOLERA
AND JILL DIED OF AMOEBIC DYSENTERY.

Harsh! But to keep things positive, the World Toilet Organization promotes November 19 as World Toilet Day. I know, it sounds funny! And it's okay with the WTO people to joke about this stuff; trust me, they expect nothing less. And after the joking, they hope people realize that Jawaharlal Nehru was right when he said, "A country in which every citizen has access to a clean toilet has reached the pinnacle of progress."

2.   Zero.

Putting Your Best Food Forward

You are a champion barfer!

This is because you eat lots of different types of foods and you are terrible at spotting the unfriendly toxins or bacteria that might be in them. (Unlike, say, your dog, you can't just sniff your food and notice that something is wrong.)

This means that humans barf WAY more than almost any other species of animal. Although this makes me proud, the problem is that our vomit is full of hydrochloric acid. That's strong stuff; it can dissolve a stainless steel spoon the way your mouth dissolves a sugar cube! So if you're constantly barfing, your strong stomach acid will damage your throat, teeth, and mouth. (And that's why it's so good to brush your teeth after puking.)

TO BARF OR NOT TO BARF . . . THAT IS THE QUESTION!

All that barfing means the human body has had to come up with a way to protect itself. And here it is: before you blow chunks, you'll start to salivate like crazy. (Many of us just go to the bathroom and start spitting into the toilet when this happens.) The saliva is being produced to protect your mouth and throat from all the acid that will soon be arriving! Yep, saliva is like a buffer between your skin and stomach acid. Who knew?! My whole life I've wondered why this happens. (Man, this book rules!)

IT'S OFFICIAL

Barfing and then having puke squirt out your nose is officially the Worst Feeling in the World.

But even though things are looking pretty bad, it's still possible to head this off at the pass. Use your mind to soothe your stomach! Take deep breaths, and try to calm down by thinking of pleasant things like rainbows, flowers, or meat loaf. (*Urp ...* okay, never mind the meat loaf.)

The challenge will be to think of *non*-gross things even as you're staring into a toilet bowl. Consider this a test of your powers of concentration! Close your eyes, breathe through your mouth, and let that cool tile floor relax your mind and body. *Ahh.* Do you feel better?

BARF-AID

To avoid barfing from motion sickness, try pushing on your wrist an inch or two down from your palm. (There are wristbands that do this for you.) This somehow "short-circuits" the barfing impulse. Hey, don't look at me. I didn't invent this system, I just report on it!

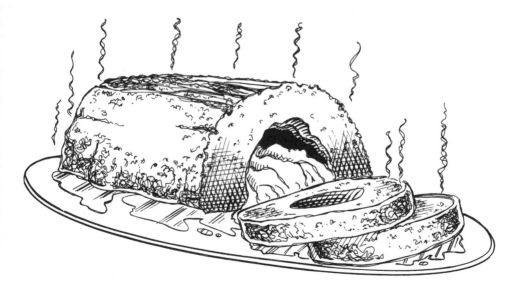

While food comes out of your stomach when you barf, your brain is the organ that puts out the red alert. That's why riding in a car on a winding road can make you ill: your body is feeling one thing (being thrown from side to side) but seeing another (the unchanging interior of the car). This is what some people call "motion sickness." And in a desperation move, the brain will decide to jettison all cargo!

If you are feeling sick in a car or on a boat, try to look at something far away that is not moving, like the horizon or the planet Jupiter. This helps calm your mind. But if you're on a roller coaster, you're pretty much out of luck. You'll be whipping around too fast to keep your eyes on much of anything! And once you start drooling and breaking out in a cold sweat, you know what's going to happen: everything must go!

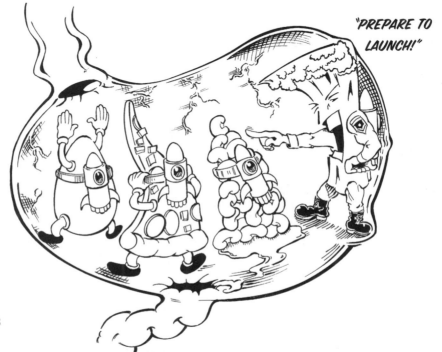

"PREPARE TO LAUNCH!"

WAYS TO SAY IT

Silly names or phrases can be a spoonful of sugar that makes the distasteful idea of barfing go down easier. Take being "bitten by Count Barf-ula," for instance. It's so stupid, it's wonderful! Other notable categories include the following:

"Ch-": For some reason, words that start with "ch-" are employed a lot when talking about vomit. So people are constantly chucking chum, Cheerios, chow, chunks, and so forth.

Democracy in Action: Bring it up for a vote.

Throwing: The popularity of "throwing up" has led to some creative phrases, such as tossing your cookies, tossing your tacos, pitching a slider, and upchucking.

Vowels Are Liquidy! Aaaaaa, Eeeeee, Iiiiii, Oooooo, Uuuuuu— and sometimes "Whhhyyy?"

Fun Combinations: Bending and sending, thunder-chunder, chowder blow, gravy gargling.

"There She Blows!": The word "blow" can be used by itself or with any colorful noun. Thus, a person can blow biscuits, soup, foam, groceries, cutlets, doughnuts, etc.

Other Favorites:

Gut-dumping, hork and beans, involuntary personal protein spill, Hyuuuundai!, buckling your stomach into the ejector seat, riding the Regurgitron, getting a round-trip meal ticket, spud spewing, yakking.

THE MAGIC TOUCH

By sticking a finger or other small item (like a feather) down their throat, a person can gag and vomit. There is some history here: in ancient Rome, the rich sometimes had huge feasts with a wide variety of food. If a Roman wanted to continue eating but was too full, he visited the vomitorium. This was an area to barf, and servants would clean up the mess. A philosopher from that time named Seneca once wrote that the Romans "vomit so that they may eat and eat so that they may vomit."

Although barfing is one of the most unpleasant things a body can do, people throughout history have tried to get some entertainment value out of it. For example, an old Viking adventure story tells of a group of travelers arriving at the home of a man named Armod Beard. Armod feeds the travelers huge amounts of a yogurt called *skyr*, and then lots of strong ale. Bad idea. The story unhurls—er, unfurls— this way:

"Egil heaves up so much vomit that it pours into Armod's face, in his eyes, up his nostrils, and into his mouth. It runs down his chest. When Armod manages to get his breath again, he then begins heaving all over. Then Egil returns to his seat and asks for more ale."

THE MORAL OF THIS STORY CAN BE EXPRESSED AS AN EQUATION: VIKING + YOGURT + ALE = TROUBLE.

Ooh, "blowing skyr" could be the new slang! And I bet that right before Egil blew skyr, he probably had those weird sensations that your body gives you to warn of an upcoming

upchucking. It turns out that there is a word for this: *vomiturient*.

★ **KECK:** To make a sound as though one is going to barf.

And vomit is still being used for entertainment purposes today. Heck, I bet that if your TV could barf, it would! The 2008 program called *Hurl* would probably bring on this response. It marked the first time in the history of television that an entire show was devoted to barf. First, the contestants stuffed themselves with food. Then they were marched onto nausea-inducing carnival rides like Loop-the-Lower Intestine and Crack the Colon. How do you win? *Don't hurl.* This was perhaps as challenging for viewers as it was for contestants. As the *Washington Post* reported, *Hurl* "oozes under the lowest bar ever set by reality television."

Speaking of barf and technology, a company named Invocon has been developing a "vomit beam" for the U.S. Navy. It shoots an invisible ray that can travel through walls and give everyone it hits dizziness and "extreme motion sickness."

This is handy, because instead of having to shoot bad people, you just aim an invisible beam at them. Then they'll fall over and puke! (You can get similar effects by cranking the volume on *American Idol.*)

POSSIBLE SILLY NAMES FOR THE WEAPON INCLUDE:

BARF: Broad Application Radio Frequency

PUKE: Personnel Usage Kinetic Energy

RALPH: Radiation Application of Long-Phase High-Energy

SPEW: Systemic Personnel Energy Weapon

SCIENCE!

Have you ever wondered why gravity doesn't keep our food down for us? I have, so I asked a doctor about it. Her response: "It's because your stomach is surrounded by a strong muscle called the diaphragm. And when that muscle heaves, contracts, and clenches, it will squish your stomach. At the same time, your food tube will relax. And then you're going to barf like there's no tomor-row." (But I don't *want* to barf like there's no tomorrow!)

So let's say you threw up and now you have the guts to look at the actual puke itself. Look, there's spaghetti! And broccoli? You don't even eat broccoli!

NAUSEA KICKS BUTT

People who throw up for a long time can sometimes get black eyes. That's because all that heaving and straining can make the small veins near their eyes burst!

In addition to the undigested and partially digested food, there will also be stomach acid and a clear, gooey stomach mucus. (The acid breaks down food, and the mucus protects your stomach from the acid.) There may be a lot more mucus in your stomach than usual when you puke. That's because, just as your body makes more saliva to protect itself, it also makes more mucus!

"THAR SHE BLOWS—CHA-CHING!!"

A family vacationing in Sydney, Australia, was enjoying some time at the beach when they made a weird discovery. A big pile of some sort of "solid fatty substance" had washed up with the surf. It turned out to be whale vomit. And since whale vomit is highly prized by the fragrance industry, the pile turned out to be worth over $200,000!

WHALE VOMIT

Smell the ADVENTURE!!

If your puke is ever green, congratulations. You managed to throw up something that's not from your stomach at all! Green barf has bile in it, and bile comes from a spot way down near your small intestine. That means you had to dig down deep for that one.

What makes bile green? It's sort of weird, but it's the same thing that makes bruises turn yellow and poop turn brown. It's a waste substance called *bilirubin*, which is made when the liver breaks down old red blood cells. Bilirubin is usually disposed of through the pooping process.

The scariest barf is called "projectile vomiting." While regular barfing involves the stomach contracting and forcing up its contents, projectile barfing is when this process happens at light speed. Additionally, a projectile vomiter's throat closes more than is normally the case, which restricts the flow of the puke. (Sort of like what happens when you put a nozzle on a hose.)

Projectile barfing is the human equivalent of shaking a can of soda. When the tab is pulled, the contents just go flying! And so with projectile vomiting, a person won't throw up at their feet. They'll throw up through a window on the other side of the room!

FAKE BARF!

There are a lot of companies that make fake barf. But the one with the best reputation is probably Chicago's Fun Inc. They make phony puke the old-fashioned way.

Actually, I guess the really old-fashioned way would be by actually puking, so never mind that!

Anyway, company president Graham Putnam says that his is "the best vomit on the market." Fair enough: it *is* a bubbly, colorful-looking pool of barf. How do they make such excellent vomit? Dunno! But I can tell you that they start with natural latex (which looks like cream) and then add chunks of colored foam.

GROSS TIP: When using fake vomit, remember that the key to faking people out is to sprinkle water on the stuff to make it look more realistic!

GROSS FLICK: Classy moviemakers sometimes need fake barf for their films. As far as I know, the most fake barf ever used in a movie was in Monty Python's *The Meaning of Life* (1983). It definitely contains the longest vomiting scene in film history. (Good grief, just *thinking* about it makes me light-headed!)

REGURGITATED ANIMAL KNOWLEDGE

Perhaps you know that many species of birds barf up food for their young. But birds aren't the only animals to do this! For example, if an adult wolf has good hunting, it will eat an incredible amount of meat and then return back to its pups. When the pups see a bulging adult wolf, they go nuts and start nibbling and poking at the adult's muzzle. This triggers a barfing reflex.

Wolf expert Dr. Gordon Haber describes the consistency of the barf as "sort of reminding me of the warm, chunky tuna sauce I used to look forward to on toast as a kid." According to the doctor, an adult wolf may barf a number of piles, and each of them can be over ten pounds!

LEARNING LESSONS FROM A CUCUMBER

The sea cucumber has much to teach us foolish humans about barfing. If threatened by a predator, one type of sea cucumber barfs its guts out. Literally! Of course, it's hard to know if it's actually barf or poop, because this sea cucumber's mouth and anus are the same hole! Anyway, this is so disgusting that the cucumber's would-be predator flees the scene. And "sea cuke puke" is so sticky and tough that people from some islands squeeze it onto their feet like a pair of shoes to protect their feet while they walk in the water!

So why is this helpful to us? Well, the sea cucumber picks an appropriate time and place to barf. If only humans could be so sensible! There's something tragic about people who *know* they're going to throw up, and then they make the worst possible decision about WHERE this horrible event will take place. For example, my sister once threw up in a floor vent. This was the *worst* possible place to do the deed! It was hard to clean out, and the smell of barf permeated the house. A slightly *better* choice would have been a sink: still messy, but at least it's close to the toilet . . . which, of course, is always the *best* choice of all (unless it's clogged!).

Here's another example. Pretend you HAD to throw up on your choice of kitchen appliances. The worst choice would probably be the waffle iron (especially if it were on!). Oh, the waffles! A blender would probably be the best place to blow. If your chowder is too chunky, you can just push the puree button!

Anyway, study these spew spot comparisons, and make the sea cucumber proud.

SPOT	WORST CHOICE	BETTER CHOICE	BEST CHOICE
School	Spewing in trombone during band class	Barfing on school bully in science class	Upchucking on kid you don't like in restroom
Car	Ashtray	Closed window, moving car	Open window, stopped car
Kitchen	Colander	Salad bowl	Dog dish
Floor Covering	Carpet	Throw rug	Throw-up rug
Laundry	Wicker wastebasket	Dirty clothes hamper	Garbage can
Sleeping	In your bed	Your brother's sock drawer	Your sister's toy box
Flying	Outer space (dry-cleaning bills for spacesuits are brutal!)	Skydiving	Airplane restroom
Hat	Sombrero	Waterproof beret	Construction worker's hard hat

SEWERS!

You're a pooping and peeing *machine*. On average, you produce 80 pounds of poop and 130 gallons of pee each year. And it takes 4,000 gallons of toilet water to flush it all away. And since billions of other people are all doing the same thing, that waste really starts to add up!

Back in prehistory, pooping and peeing was no big deal. There weren't that many people around! So the hunter-gatherers and nomads could just poop and keep walking.

But as soon as people started building small settlements, they had a problem. They didn't want to poop right by their homes! So before a person pooped, he put one foot in front of the other and took a walk away from the village. As one ancient document suggested, "Shoot an arrow from your home. Do not poop any closer to it than where the arrow lands." (That's almost a direct quote.)

Eventually, people started hanging out in larger and larger groups. Pretty soon, we had cities! This posed a problem. If you lived in a large city, you couldn't just walk until you got to the wilderness. You'd have to walk all day! So the ancient Greeks and Romans used plumbing and running water to remove poop. Since individual flush toilets weren't available, people got together in public bathrooms called *forica*, where they could sit on marble seats in rows and socialize.

For societies without plumbing, "cesspits" were a solution. The idea was to dig a hole. Now put all your pee and poop into it! But the pee and poop liquids would seep into the soil. This was bad if the people drew drinking water from nearby! That's how deadly diseases like cholera (which hides in human poop) get spread.

But cesspits could be lined with stone so that their sewage stayed put. And if a society were really organized, every so often, someone would come in to clean out (or "muck") the cesspit. But who was going to do that dirty work? In France, a cesspit cleaner was called the *Maître Fifi*. He'd show up with his crew in the dead of night with carts, shovels, hoists, pulleys, and, most importantly, big buckets. And you didn't mess with the *Maître Fifi*. If you made fun of his job title or didn't pay your bill on time, he had a weapon to use on you: your own poop! (He might use it to smear "Pay your bills" on the walls of your house, for instance.)

In India, a different method was used. For thousands of years, India's social system had five basic levels. At the top were the Brahmins, and at the bottom were the Dalits, also known as the Untouchables. Among other nasty jobs, the Dalits were in charge of burning dead bodies and handling human poop. To protest this unfairness, Mohandas Gandhi (who was a Brahmin) made a point of cleaning his own cesspit. This came as a great shock to his fellow Indians!

As for Americans, they originally had to take care of their own poop with a private sewer or outhouse. But city-dwellers got a breakthrough in the 1870s. That's when cities began putting in big sewage systems for everyone to share. That was good news!

SECURITY ALERT!

Sewer lines are big enough to allow people (and killer robots!) to move through them. So the sewers that pass by high-security zones like Buckingham Palace, the White House, and my house have sensors in them. If the sensors are triggered, police are alerted that an assassin or ice cream salesperson might be sneaking through them.

There have been a number of historical figures who could have used this system. In the 1400s, King James of Scotland was ambushed in his bathroom by murderous nobles. And a murderous monk stabbed French King Henri III while he was taking care of his royal business in 1589. Worst of all was the fate of Japanese warlord Uesugi Kenshin, who was enjoying a private moment when he was attacked from below by a ninja assassin who'd been hiding in the toilet's cesspit for days!

163

But let's get back to *you*. Unless your home has a septic tank, everything that gets flushed will hook up with the run-off water from your shower and the kitchen sink. This wastewater runs out of your home to the sewer, where it joins the rainwater (and anything else) running down street drains.

And ALL of it is piped to a "wastewater-treatment plant." Before we get there, maybe we should take a little field trip into the sewer. But first, you have to be prepared!

GOING INTO THE SEWER? BE READY!

Before climbing down into the dark world of the sewers, you'll need:

★ A hard hat with a miner's light
★ Rubber hip waders
★ Heavy rubber gloves
★ Overalls
★ An emergency breathing device (in case you hit pockets of poisonous gas)
★ A walkie-talkie to communicate with your back-up team
★ A spear gun for the rats (*kidding!*)

Even though you're pretty well covered, try not to touch anything while you're in the sewer. Hepatitis, typhoid, cholera, and many other bacteria and viruses live down there.

Also, don't make any sparks! Sewers have methane in them, and you know that's flammable. It would be pretty stinky to get caught in a huge poop fireball!

Okay, you're at the bottom of the sewer line. It's a dark, moist, underground world down here! Be careful not to get

AND YOU THOUGHT OVERFLOWING TOILETS WERE BAD!

Sewer systems often overflow when it rains. That puts raw sewage right into your nearest stream, river, or harbor. For example, New York averages fifty million gallons of sewage overflow every week!

lost. Some sewer systems, like the one under London, are so colossal that they haven't been fully explored since they were built.

Now you're ready to see the sights! In addition to water, pee, and poop, you'll find everything that people can flush down a toilet or run down a storm drain: dead tropical fish, hair, lint, soap, diapers, toothpaste, leaves, Q-tips, razor blades, needles, and hundreds and hundreds of cell phones. And there are also drain cleaners, weed killer, and baby shampoo (*Nooo!*) to worry about.

If you're trying to guess the scariest thing you'll see, "grease" is the word! When restaurants and people cooking at home need to get rid of used cooking oil and grease, many just pour it down the drain. In the sewer, the grease will collect and solidify until it turns into a fatty, impenetrable wall that clogs everything. (*Nooo!*)

NOW, THAT'S GROSS

Worldwide, about 90 percent of all human sewage gets dumped straight into the ocean. This creates dead zones where no marine life can exist. There are currently more than four hundred of these.

But WAIT—I just got some bad news! Rainy weather is coming. That means you need to get out of the sewer quickly. Sudden rainfall can turn a nice, quiet sewer into a raging torrent of rainwater in no time flat. (That is, the sewer will fill up in no time, and you'll be knocked flat!)

After you get all of your sewer gear off, it's time to catch a ride with your mom to the wastewater plant. First, the brown water in the sewer flows through screens that filter out the big stuff. Any poop that's still in one piece will get crushed right through these, but anything that shouldn't be in the water (like water bottles and Q-tips) or any food that wasn't digested (like corn kernels) can get caught here.

The first city sewers just dumped all the poop and pee into the nearest river, lake, or ocean. Not good! But the brown wastewater from your sewer is pumped into a giant tank or pool and left alone. This is so the solid waste in it can sink to the bottom and the grease and fat will float to the top as scum. Nice!

Leaving the solid waste and scum behind, the water is pumped out to holding tanks. Oxygen is then piped into the water to help bacteria break down its remaining organic wastes. As oxygen is pumped in, the brown water bubbles, and it looks like chocolate mousse.

If the bacteria do their job, the once-brown water will eventually become clear. But it's still polluted! Some wastewater plants will now pipe this water into the nearest brook, river, lake, or ocean. But the *good* wastewater plants will filter this water through sand and then shoot it with ultraviolet rays of light, which kill any harmful germs still hanging around.

Two things come out of a wastewater treatment system: clean water (*yay!*) and the sludge that's made up of all the pollution and gunk that's been filtered out of the water (*blech!*). This sludgy stuff—called "biosolids"—is nasty, and getting rid of it is a problem. Until 1998, U.S. plants could just dump the sludge at sea. Nowadays, the sludge sometimes gets burned and sometimes buried. And if the sludge is treated properly, a good use for it is as fertilizer.

SEPTIC TANK?

If your home's plumbing isn't hooked up to a sewer system, then you probably have a septic tank somewhere nearby. This is a big underground tank that all of your family's waste flows into through a pipe. The solids sink to the bottom of the tank. As for the liquids, they usually sit in the tank for a while before getting leaked back into the nearby soil (aka, "septic field").

So if you have a septic tank, at some point someone's going to need to come and muck it out! This involves big trucks, big vacuums, and big hoses.

When I was a kid, we had a septic tank, and I remember
the first time a guy came to vacuum it out. I'd never realized there was a huge tank right under home plate on our
backyard's Whiffleball field! When the guy opened the lid,
he laughed. There was a thick, solid crust of grease that
had formed over the top of the tank's contents! (Remember,
grease floats.) He had to take a crowbar and break through
the grease crust before he could start vacuuming the solids
out. And as soon as he broke that crust, it *really* stank!

IT WAS SO BAD THAT AFTER HE LEFT, WE MOVED HOME
BASE!

GROSS ANATOMY

The human body is gross enough when it's actually *healthy*. So as you can imagine, some of the things that can go wrong with us are pretty horrendous. But don't worry—I'm not going to write about someone having a three-hundred-pound cyst removed from his nostril. Look, there are entire series of books dedicated to all the major illnesses that a person could get, and this isn't one of them!

So, instead, why don't you take a couple of deep breaths and say "Aaaaahhh"? After that, we can warm up with a few junior illnesses.

First up is a nose infection called *rhinitis caseosa*. The medical dictionary says that when someone gets this, the nasal cavities "are more or less completely filled with a foul-smelling cheesy material." Wow! Apparently, this nose cheese is teeming with nasty bacteria and germs. Then pus gets added to the mucus, and it starts smelling really bad. Yes, the nose stinks! In some cases, a doctor may have to remove over three inches of "foul-smelling cheese" from the nose just to clear the sinuses.

But medications help cure *rhinitis caseosa*, so it's not considered dangerous. Just gross!

BUT I DON'T WANT TO LIVE IN A GRAVEYARD!

Settlers built Louisville, Kentucky, on top of ponds. The ponds had lots of mosquitoes. The mosquitoes had lots of diseases. This led to one of Louisville's first nicknames: the Graveyard of the West.

GROSS-SOUNDING PARTS OF THE BODY!

GLABELLA: *The area between the eyebrows.*

NASION: *The spot where the top of the nose touches the bottom of the glabella.*

RHINARIUM: *The area around the nostrils.*

FRENULUM: *The small ridge of tissue attached beneath the tongue and between the lips and gums.*

GINGLYMUS: *A hinge joint, such as the inner elbow.*

ANATOMICAL SNUFFBOX: *The deepening part of the outside of the wrist formed when you raise your thumb.*

CANTHUS: *The outer or inner corner of the eye, where the lids meet.*

PHILTRUM: *The space between the upper lip and nose.*

STERNOHYOI *A muscle in front of the throat.*

XYPHOID PROCESS: *A chunk of cartilage at the bottom-center of the sternum.*

BURSA SAC: *A fluid-filled sac.*

PHALANX: *A bone of the finger or toe.*

172

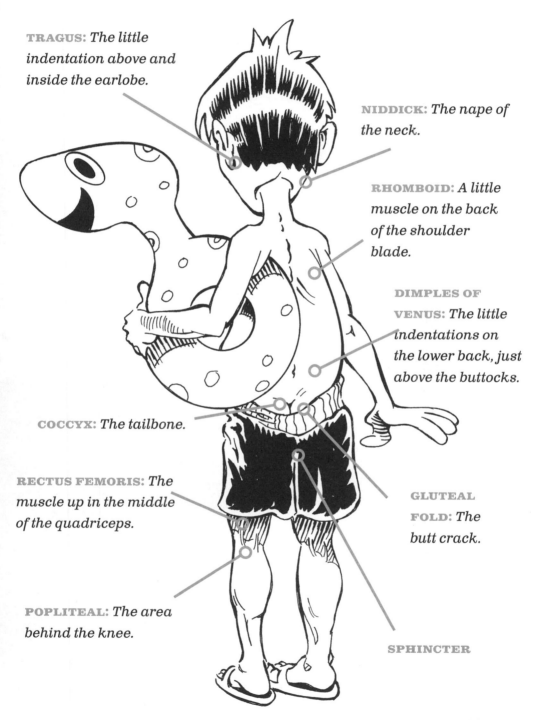

TRAGUS: *The little indentation above and inside the earlobe.*

NIDDICK: *The nape of the neck.*

RHOMBOID: *A little muscle on the back of the shoulder blade.*

DIMPLES OF VENUS: *The little indentations on the lower back, just above the buttocks.*

COCCYX: *The tailbone.*

RECTUS FEMORIS: *The muscle up in the middle of the quadriceps.*

GLUTEAL FOLD: *The butt crack.*

POPLITEAL: *The area behind the knee.*

SPHINCTER

THE TOAST FROM OUTER SPACE

Eyes are made out of jelly. *Eye jelly.* Doesn't that strike you as a little strange? You can *see* out of two dabs of jelly! And there are huge holes behind the dabs, which means that, theoretically, you could be scratching your eye, your finger could slip, and then your finger would plunge into your brain!

I'm just saying.

What if aliens came to earth and wanted to use our eye jelly to spread on their toast? There would only be ONE way to save the human race, and here it is:

WE WOULD HAVE TO LET OUR GOUND BUILD UP.

Huh? You don't know what gound is? Then we're all doomed ... unless you keep reading and learn that gound is the dried mucus that builds up around your eyes while you sleep. Let's see how those stinking Martians like some of our eye snot on their

TWTHTBG: TRYING WAY TOO HARD TO BE GROSS

An Indian man named B. Y. Tyagi the longest ear hair in the world It's four inches long—and still growing!

toast! And if they try to switch to bagels, our bed boogers still aren't going to taste ANY better!

You also have tiny spider-like organisms living in your eyes. That's right, there are follicle mites living in your eyelashes. But the grossest thing about eyes are worms ... eye worms! These one-to-two-inch-long worms, known as the Loa Loa, are able migrate around the body's tissues. If a Loa Loa decides to cruise into an eyeball, a person can feel (and see!) the worm fairly easily!

But unless you live in Central Africa, you don't have to worry about getting these. *Whew!*

While eye worms are rare, some medical problems are simply one of a kind. The most bizarre story I've heard lately is of a Russian man who complained of chest pain. Doctors went in to investigate, and they found a five-centimeter-long spruce tree (complete with green needles) growing in the man's lung!

The doctors were stumped by what they saw. (Get it?[1]) They assumed a tree seed had somehow gotten into the moist confines of the man's lung and started to grow! So they got out a chainsaw—*kidding!* They surgically removed the tree from the man's lung, sewed him back up, and told him to stop inhaling spruce seeds.

1. "Stumped"!

When it comes to having surgery, you might think that hearing the doctors say, "Crikey! He's got a spruce tree growing in his lung" would be the last thing you'd want to hear from the operating table. But there might be something even worse, like perhaps:

"I AM NOW TRANSPLANTING THE PATIENT'S BRAIN INTO THIS ORANGUTAN'S SKULL."

SCROFULA AND LEPROSY

Some diseases have such disgustingly cool names, you just have to take notice. Like scrofula! This disease causes large glandular swellings in the neck. (Nasty!) And it even has a cool nickname: the King's Evil.[2] (That's because it was once believed that a touch from a king could cure the disease. How's that for scientific?)

But not to worry. In the very unlikely event that you were to get scrofula, it's treatable with modern antibiotics. But a disease you wouldn't ever be able to get rid of is leprosy,

2.   Of course, by reading this book, you already *have* the King's Evil.

BUT DID IT HURT?

In 1996, a Missouri woman sued her county government after she fell in an icy school parking lot. According to her lawsuit: "All the bones, organs, muscles, tendons, tissues, nerves, veins, arteries, ligaments ... discs, cartilages, and the joints of her body were fractured, broken, ruptured, punctured, compressed, dislocated, separated, bruised, contused, narrowed, abrased, lacerated, burned, cut, torn, wrenched, swollen, strained, sprained, inflamed, and infected."

which causes your skin to get thicker while your nerves die off. Then your "extremities" (the parts of your body farthest from your heart) get numb and rot. Sometimes they fall off. As the disease worsens, you can lose your fingers, toes, nose, eyebrows, and even bigger pieces of yourself.

Since leprosy can be contagious, "lepers" have historically been discriminated against. In parts of Europe during the Middle Ages, they could be denied inheritances, and they weren't allowed to walk narrow streets because they'd get too close to other people. And on top of all that, putting

"Leper" on your business card is not going to impress anyone.

There are names even more gross-sounding than scrofula or leprosy. For instance, how about *blepharitis*? I had this once, and it was so horrible, I can't share its symptoms with you, even in a book like this![3]

THE CURIOUS CASE OF BENJAMIN BUTTON'S SCARS

While scars usually heal up nicely, sometimes they can go backward in time! Here's how:

Scurvy is a disease that sailors used to get due to a lack of vitamin C. What happens if you have scurvy is the "glue" that holds the body together starts to vanish. First, a scurvy victim gets loose teeth, rotten gums, and joint pain. Then scabs stop healing and actually turn back into open wounds. Finally, old scars open up and healed broken bones break again! Scurvy used to be so common among sailors that a third of a ship's crew often fell victim to it as late as 1800.

3.   Okay, okay, it's an inflamed eyelid.

SCABS AND BRUISES

ook, I don't know how you got that scab in the first place. Maybe your sister came after you with a butter knife after you teased her about her shoelaces. Or maybe your dog stuck a spork in your lymph node because you wouldn't play Fetch.

All I know is what happened after you got cut. First, you were bleeding. *Downer!* That always seems to happen. I used to wonder if there were a little spot on the body without any blood vessels. But it turns out that if you take a gentle pinch of the skin anywhere on your body, there are about three feet of little blood vessels in there!

So if you get cut, you're going to bleed.

But since a cut could let outside bacteria directly into your body, you need some kind of defense. And so a number of unusual blood cells named platelets arrive on the scene. They form a circle around your cut and start turning from liquid to jelly to a solid. As your blood clots, a scab is formed. Thanks, platelets!

Your face has so many blood vessels, however, that even healthy platelets can have a hard time healing a cut there. This is too bad for mixed-martial-arts fighters. They tend to get punched in the face a lot, so they are at high risk for having facial cuts. To avoid losing a match because of this, many of these tough guys turn to plastic surgery.

This is where corpses come in! First, dead skin is taken from a dead body. (What other kind of skin could it be?) Then a surgeon opens up the skin in the fighter's face and removes any scar tissue, usually around the eyes. A one-square-centimeter piece of donor skin is then placed in the opening and stitched back over! Amazingly, the dead-skin implant then gets absorbed back into the patient's own skin. And the odds are much lower for getting a cut on the same spot again.

Bad news! If you do get cut, you really shouldn't let a vampire bat lick the wound. You see, these bats have an anti-coagulant in their spit that keeps a cut from scabbing up. (This allows the bat to keep drinking from an animal's blood until the bat is nice and full.)

Once your cut has scabbed up, you may notice that it shrinks over time, causing some pinching of the skin. It's almost like your body is trying to sew the wound back together. This is also likely to cause some itching to occur. It's no coincidence that "scab" has its roots in the Latin word *scabere*: to scratch!

"This is all very interesting," you say, "but where do scars come from?" Well, if your dog really twisted that spork into you, this cut might be so deep that even a hard-working scab can't repair all the damage. In a case like this, the body has to form special connective tissue to take care of the problem. And after the flesh heals, it won't look the same as it did before the injury, but at least you'll have a cool spork scar.

We've covered what happens when a blood vessel gets cut. But what if it gets *squished* instead? For instance, if a baseball drills you in the thigh, your blood vessels will get crushed. The impact from the ball literally bursts the blood vessels inside your body, which causes internal bleeding. The result: a bruise!

A bruise usually starts out purple, or even greenish-blue. As your body sends white blood cells to the bruise to clean up the bloody mess, the bruise will change color to a strange type of yellow. I think the best kinds of bruises are the ones you can share with the world. Let's say you're playing basketball and you get elbowed in the face. That's a good way to pick up a black eye, which is just a facial bruise. As it heals, everyone will get to see the bruise go through more color changes than a chameleon on a kaleidoscope!

MEDICAL STUDENTS: WHAT A BUNCH OF CUT-UPS!

When it comes to treating human suffering, medical professionals are our front line of defense. Our doctors and nurses deal with life's important stuff. Yes, it may be gross, but that's not what's important. So thank goodness these angels of medical mercy have studied up on how to treat the problems that afflict us all.

Of course, there's something very wrong with these people. Who would *want* to study grotesque horrors? For example, let's look at the logical, precise way doctors are taught today. Imagine a group of medical students walking into a classroom. The one I have in mind is known as the gross anatomy lab, or "gross lab" for short. (Seriously.) The classroom is already set up with rows of decapitated human heads sitting on roasting pans.

USING THESE HEADS, THE MEDICAL STUDENTS WILL PRACTICE THE SURGICAL PROCEDURES THAT THEY WILL ONE DAY PERFORM ON LIVING DECAPITATED HEADS.

WITHOUT PUS WE WOULDN'T HAVE PUSTULES!

White blood cells, or leukocytes, are your first line of defense against bacteria and other germs. They're like gang members cruising your bloodstream, looking for trouble. If the white blood cells find a germ, they gang up on the organism and a brawl breaks out.

Your white blood cells try to eat the germ, and of course the germ fights back. In the course of battle, some of your white blood cells are killed. Poor little fellers! Their dead bodies form a liquid we call pus. This is sort of cool when you think about it. Your pus comes from your own dead soldiers!

Wait, that's not right! Gross lab is where medical students learn all about human anatomy, and in order to do so, they cut apart and examine dead human bodies, or cadavers. The cadavers are all people who have volunteered their bodies to science. As the beginning students get started, they are often paired off with each other and given an entire body to work with. The first thing the students do is roll the body onto its stomach. That way, cutting up the body seems less personal, and it also makes it easier for students to get used to touching a dead body.

BAD DOG!
GIVE MOMMY THE NOSE!

An Italian woman named Loredana Romano was once dissected by her poodle.

But don't worry, this story has a happy ending!

Romano's dog was named Vale, and Vale was allowed to jump into Romano's bed. But one day everything went horribly wrong. After the dog jumped into bed with her, Romano reported that Vale "suddenly bit off my nose."

Afterward, Vale ran off with the nose. Italian police officers chased the dog around Romano's garden until they finally retrieved the nose, which doctors reattached to Romano's face. The dog was forgiven. Clearly, Vale had been curious to see how easily a nose could come off someone's face. (Answer: pretty easily.)

But Vale is NOT allowed up on the bed anymore. (So I guess I was wrong. The story doesn't have a happy ending after all!)

Rolling the body over and seeing its face is always a jolt. But within a couple of days, the students have cut their person down to size with bone saws and very sharp instruments. It takes an hour of sawing and chiseling to remove the top of the skull. Students say that when the skullcap comes off, it sounds like a big piece of Velcro being torn. And they say the brain feels kind of like a water balloon filled with gelatin.

Although today's doctors are very well informed, for most of human history, people had no clear ideas about what was inside the body. And since almost everyone had rules against dissecting humans, our learning curve has been pretty slow. There was one brief historical period when the ban on dissections was lifted, and Herophilus of Alexandria (335–280 BCE) took full advantage of it. There was just one catch: Herophilus preferred to dissect *living* people. (This is called vivisection.) He may have cut open as many as six hundred lucky prisoners who involuntarily donated their bodies to science.

So is Herophilus remembered as a mass-murdering mad scientist? *Puh-leeze!* Don't dis the man known as the "Father of Anatomy."

But open season on human dissections ended pretty fast, and from then on, doctors pursuing knowledge had to pursue dead bodies in secret. As you can imagine, this hobby

completely freaked people out. These doctors were known as body snatchers! Ghouls! Grave robbers!

As a public relations move, the good doctors invented a different word for what they were doing: resurrectionists! No dice. Even executioners had better reputations than doctors who were interested in anatomy.

A successful grave robber's worst enemy was time. In a world without refrigeration, bodies decomposed quickly. In fact, as with sports like baseball or basketball, dissection had a "season": the cold months when bodies would keep for a longer period!

In response to grave robbers, coffin-makers came up with a number of techniques to prevent the theft of bodies. Here are three of my favorites:

★ **THE MORTSAFE:** Imagine a combination of a coffin and a safe, complete with a reinforced door and a combination lock.

★ **THE NESTING COFFIN:** In this scenario, a grave robber would open a coffin, only to find another coffin inside. Getting THAT coffin open would reveal ... yet another coffin! (By this time, the frustrated grave robber would leave in disgust.)

★ **CORPSE STRAPS:** The body is lowered into the coffin and then strapped into place with several metal straps.

The most famous body snatcher was a man named William Burke. After selling a corpse to a doctor, Burke decided to skip the distasteful "digging up graves" part of the job. It seemed easier just to murder people instead, and so that's what he did. Sixteen times! After being caught, convicted, and hung, Burke's body was used for—wait for it—dissection. His skeleton is still in Edinburgh's Royal College of Surgeons.[4]

"GROSS, DUDE!" HALL OF FAME

William Harvey (1578–1657) published groundbreaking books on the human circulatory system. How did he learn so much about the topic? Lots of dissections, including ones on his sister and father!

4. And for some reason, they made wallets out of Burke's skin. Really.

RELICS!

Have you ever seen a professional basketball player fling his jersey (or headband) into the stands at the end of a game? Fans go crazy! They lunge for the sweat-soaked clothing like it was a precious garment from on high.

While we might call that headband a souvenir today, in another time, it might have been called a "relic." But whatever you call it, the desire to get something that once belonged to a celebrity is a strong one. In the old days, any part of a noteworthy person's body or belongings was considered valuable. This was especially true of saints and other holy people.

EVEN THE WHOLE BODY OF THE FAMOUS PERSON COULD BE THE RELIC THAT PEOPLE WANTED.

Let me give you an example. John the Baptist is a famous Christian figure who had his head chopped off. And if you're looking for John's head today, you can find it in TWO places: Istanbul and Damascus! You can see the problem. These types of relics are often fake, but that hasn't stopped people from wanting them.

In the thirteenth century, an Englishman named Hugh of Lincoln was in charge of building a new church. In order to give his church some street cred, Hugh was anxious to get his hands on a relic. So he went to a monastery in France where the arm of Mary Magdelene was supposedly kept in a casket. (Why did they have her arm? *It was a relic!*)

When Hugh saw the arm, he was overcome with devotion. He leaned into the casket to kiss the relic. And with his head in there, he opened his jaw and BIT a piece of Mary's leathery arm off! His plan was to return home with the mouthful of Mary to use as his own church's relic. But he was caught! Man, was he in trouble.

Hugh was allowed to speak in his own defense, and he said that if Catholics eat communion wafers, and if communion were believed to be part of God, why couldn't he take a bite out of a mere saint? While this may sound like a stretch to you, it convinced Hugh's captors. They let him go, and he took with him his piece of the relic.

The bodies of certain saints, like that of St. Francis Xavier, were cut up into various pieces to serve as relics in far-flung churches. Some holy people made plans *before* their death to help make this happen. Before the Buddha died, he charged a monk to go through his cremated remains and save anything that was salvageable (ashes, bone, teeth) to spread among the faithful.

Now *that's* thoughtfulness!

BELLY BUTTONS

As far as I can tell, belly buttons were invented so that lint would have a place to hang out. Scientists have studied belly button lint (seriously), and here are some results of their very important research:

★ Belly button lint is composed of dust, dried sweat, fat, dead skin, and bits of cotton.

★ These items usually gather around the belly button before being drawn into it.

★ The hairs near the belly button grow in circles around it. This helps direct bits of lint into it.

★ People with hairless bellies collect much less lint than those with hairy ones.

★ The person most likely to have a ton of gunk in his belly button is a fat, middle-aged hairy man. (And that's only the *second*-grossest thing in this chapter.)

GRAHAM'S CRACKERS

A man named Graham Barker has collected his belly button lint in jars since 1984.

To get the inside story on your belly button, we have to go back to when you were in your mother's

DON'T THEY TEACH KIDS ANYTHING?

Paramedics responded to a 911 call made by a thirteen-year-old boy. He reported that his guts were falling out! When the paramedics got to him, the boy told them that "stuff" was coming out of his belly button. This "stuff" was belly button lint.

womb. There wasn't any air to breathe in there! So all of your oxygen went through the umbilical cord that connected to the spot where your belly button is now. (This cord also brought you nutrition and carried away some of your waste.)

In other words, you "breathed" through the hole where your belly button is today!

After you were born, the doctor cut your umbilical cord. This means that your belly button is the first scar you ever got, left over from your first surgery! So if you see a woman showing off her belly button with a short blouse or top, you can politely remind her that it's actually a scar. (I'm sure she'll appreciate the thought.)

When a person is seated, their belly skin may fold over their belly button. It depends on whether or not the person is overweight. If the belly button is constantly folded under a crease of fat, then it's going to be warm, dark, and moist most of the time. This can lead to a yeasty fungus infection! When this happens, the belly button gets a cheesy, moldy substance in it. A common form of this infection is called *candida fungi*, which is the same thing that gives babies diaper rash.

But extremely overweight people can get infections anywhere their flesh is hanging. There are plenty of horror stories about the yeasty skin infections hiding in the gigantic skin flaps of obese people. And I'm not going to tell you any of them! Now go get some exercise.

THE APPENDIX: AS USEFUL AS A SCREEN DOOR ON A SUBMARINE

The appendix usually comes at the end of a book, but I was born a rebel, so I'm putting it here. (Ah, book humor.)

BUT WHAT ABOUT THE HUMAN APPENDIX? IF YOU WERE TO TAKE A VOYAGE INTO YOUR STOMACH, THROUGH YOUR SMALL INTESTINE, AND ONWARD INTO YOUR BIG INTESTINE, YOU'D HAVE TWO THOUGHTS:

First, you'd wonder what you're doing in your own digestive system. (Never mind that!)

Next, you'd wonder about a duct you'd see in the side of the large intestine. See it? It's the one discharging stinky greenish-yellow fluid. Does this horrible liquid help digest food? Nope. Does this discharge have any use at all?

Nope.

Welcome to the world of your appendix! It's just a dead-end tube coming off your large intestine. And it makes stinky, useless fluid. Oh, and it's also dangerous. The appendix can get infected, fill with pus, and begin to swell up in a painful condition known as appendicitis. And if that swollen appendix isn't removed, it will burst and release infected grossness into the body. This is NOT good, and if not treated immediately, it can lead to MAJOR problems. (FYI, a common warning sign of appendicitis is a pain around the belly button. This pain then shifts to the lower-right side of the body and is *very* tender.)

PUS: IT'S WHAT'S FOR DINNER

What follows could be the most disgusting thing in this whole book. (Consider that a warning.)

St. Catherine of Siena, who lived in the 1300s, once nursed a woman with a dreadful growth on her body. No one else would do the job because pus and horrible odors came out of this growth. But even though Catherine took excellent care of the afflicted woman, she was ashamed that the ailment could so disgust her. So to overcome her disgust and to show her religious devotion, Catherine apparently collected the pus coming out of the growth and drank it.

Hey, how do you think she became a saint? If there is something to like about this horrifying story, it's that even the most disgusting situation can bring out the best in people.

Now if you'll excuse me, I have to go lie down.

It's a Gross World, After All!

"IT'S HARD TO DEFINE GROSS BECAUSE IT WILL OFTEN VARY FROM ONE CULTURE TO THE NEXT. BUT WHAT IS CONSTANT IS THAT EACH CULTURE WILL FIND SOMETHING DISGUSTING. IT'S ONE OF THE PRIMARY FEATURES OF ANY CIVILIZATION."

—WILLIAM I. MILLER, THE ANATOMY OF DISGUST

All across the planet, people show their disgust by making a "scrunched-up" face. But why do we all do that? Some scientists think the reason we squint our eyes and scrunch up our noses is because this helps screen out nasty-looking and nasty-smelling stuff. So when you make the disgusted face, you see less and you smell less. That's handy!

But there are many differences between how grossness is defined from one place to the next. For example, an international survey about what various countries find to be gross revealed this:

LOCATION	THING THAT GROSSES THEM OUT
India	Kissing in public; other people's clothes
Great Britain	Dead sparrows; cruelty to horses; eating bugs
The Netherlands	Dog saliva; politicians
Athens International Airport	Wet people; being eaten alive by insects

This raises an interesting question: What's wrong with wet people, and why don't Greeks like them? Oh well, I suppose some things will never be known!

There are good reasons to be disgusted by some things (pus, anyone?), but people also freak out in illogical ways. For example, I am sort of sickened by confetti and other really small pieces of paper. And if they get wet (like spitballs), it absolutely grosses me out.

But if I were to get enough people to agree with me about this, it wouldn't seem slightly odd to be a freak about wet confetti. It would be normal!

The main thing that changes from country to country is what gets defined as "cooties." This is the idea that if something gross touches something normal, the normal thing somehow becomes infected. Another word for this is *contamination*.

Based on my research, India is one of the most contamination-fearing cultures in the world. The idea of wearing the laundered clothes of another person is disgusting to millions of Indians, because the "essence" of the person is still in the threads. And Americans and Europeans are generally not interested in eating insects, though enjoying a handful of termites is no big deal to many folks living in South America, Australia, and Africa.

One thing that humans everywhere agree on is that if something is really gross, you just want to get away from it. This helps explain why people who want to express strong anger or disgust sometimes will throw a disgusting thing AT someone else. For example, some politicians get eggs thrown at them by their opponents. (Sadly, in my family, it can also be a way of saying, "We love you.")

It was not always widely known that showing someone the sole of your shoe is a deep insult in the

LIGHTS, CAMERA, FART!

The Swedish word for "action" is "fart."

Middle East. Shoes are viewed as being somewhat disgusting there, since a person might have stepped in anything! But after an Iraqi journalist threw his shoe at the U.S. president in 2008, this way of looking at shoes became more well-known. Soon, copycat shoe-throwers in China and Israel tried their hand at this expression of disgust.

This led me to wonder about other kinds of stuff people throw to show their displeasure. Here's one from Canada! In 2007, a school principal was suspended for throwing poop at a twelve-year-old kid who was bothering her.

Human poop.

Okay, I'm done.

FRENCH POOP

There's a place in Paris called *Le Musée de la Poupée.* Wow! A whole museum devoted to poop?! I had to see that.

So you can imagine my disappointment when I traveled there and found that it's actually a museum of dolls. But since I was in France anyway, I decided to learn a little more about the French and their poop.

Probably the weirdest thing I found out was that in the 1700s, French noblewomen used a special snuff called *poudrette*. Snuff is usually made of powdered tobacco that is inhaled quickly up the nose. But the main ingredient of *poudrette* was dried, powdered human poop.

IT WAS INHALED QUICKLY UP THE NOSE.

Yikes! The French seem to have a healthy relationship with poop. For example, more than three hundred years ago, King Louis xiv liked to receive diplomatic visitors while he was pooping. (Maybe he inspired U.S. president Lyndon B. Johnson, who did the same thing with reporters and his staff.) But even so, the worst insult the former emperor of France, Napoleon Bonaparte, could think of was, "He is a silk stocking filled with dung."

France is thought of as having a refined and civilized culture. This can make people think the French are snobs. Even the French sometimes think they're snobs! Take French wine, for example. Jean-Marc Speziale is a French winemaker who heard one too many times from his countrymen that the wine from his region of the country tasted like *merde* (poop).

So Jean-Marc started bottling his own wine: *Le vin de merde*, or "wine of the poop." (The label on the bottle shows a large fly at the top right-hand corner!)

THE SKIN YOU'RE IN

You've got guts.

And that's why you should rejoice in your skin! After all, your skin is the only thing keeping all of the oozing, pulsating guts and goop inside you from slopping into a big wet pile on the ground. (Boy, that was a fun sentence to write!)

And if you think about what's underneath it, your skin is your least disgusting feature. But we're more self-conscious about our skin than, say, our lungs. That's because everyone can see our skin. So even though it's not very gross, if our skin gets a little rash or a teensy zit, or maybe a medium-

size cyst or boil, we freak out and think we look worse than
we actually do.

Hey, have you ever noticed that if you scratch a bug bite
too much, your fingernails can raise a welt on your skin?
Me too! There's a woman named Ariana Page Russell who
has such sensitive skin, it will immediately swell up at the
slightest scratch. Then the skin shrinks back down pretty
quickly. Because of this superpower, Russell calls herself
"the human Etch A Sketch" and actually scratches patterns
on herself to create art. Then she takes pictures of the art
and sells it. Good for the human Etch A Sketch for being
creative with her skin condition!

Since you're a mammal, you have hairs sticking out of your
body. (If you are NOT a mammal, please e-mail me a descrip-
tion of what you actually are!) At the root (or *follicle*) of each
hair are two or more oil glands. These glands are in charge
of keeping your hair lubricated with oil. That's why your
hair gets oily even if you don't go outside at all.

Most teenagers find that their bodies are making way more
oil than before. (This is because their bodies are making
hormones called androgens.) More oil? Not good! This oil
traps dirt and also starts drying. This gunky mess can block
the sweat pores of your skin. Pretty soon a lump forms.
This lump is called a *comedo*, but it's not funny. It's from
a Latin word meaning "fat maggot." Uncool! The comedo

might turn into a blackhead, which is a zit with a black head. (*Duh!*) Squeezing the blackhead will often push out a tendril of yellow wax. *Blech!* That's the dried grease that got trapped in your skin.

BIZARRE BEZOARS

When a cat licks its fur, some of the fur goes into its mouth and gets swallowed. But hair can't be digested, so it just sits in the cat's stomach, waiting for other hairs to join it. And at some point, the ball is big enough to get yacked up!

If you think that's bad, *human* hairballs are much worse. Some people—usually young people with long hair—develop the nervous habit of hair chewing. And just like cats, a hairball forms, but with humans we call them *bezoars*. While the stomach can't digest this hairball, it can turn it into what looks like an odd-looking rock. In fact, people used to think that bezoars *were* rocks. They were believed to have magic properties and were even used as an antidote for poison.

What about whiteheads? Gee, I was hoping you wouldn't ask. The recipe for this classic zit calls for a blocked sweat gland that's infected with bacteria. Your immune system sends white blood cells to the area to take care of the germs. A nice little soup of pus is made, and *ta-dah!* A zit is born!

Since teen boys make ten times the amount of androgens as teen girls, boys are ten times more likely to get really bad acne.

BAD SKIN, BOILS, AND COMMUNISM!

A colossal zit is called a *sebaceous cyst.* These can be an inch or more across! And because of their size, they can leave permanent craters behind if someone tries to pop them. So leave the cysts to the experts. A doctor will carefully lance the cyst. This is extremely gross. I observed it once, and the cyst actually made a deep popping sound!

If you think a cyst is serious, you're right. The only thing worse is a *boil,* which is a super-cyst. And if a bunch of boils grow near each other and connect up, that's called a *carbuncle.* It's one of the worst things that can happen to your skin. Let's just say that it involves a lot of pain, swelling, and pus. And when a carbuncle pops, the skin over it comes right off and is replaced by an open sore.

The writer Karl Marx came up with a social system called Communism, in which everyone would share property and get paid based on what they actually needed. But according to Marx, in order for the system to get started, there first had to be a war between the rich and the poor.

If this sounds like a bad way to start a new society, I should mention that Marx suffered from extremely painful boils for most of his life. Unfortunately, he had a skin disease called *Hidradenitis suppurativa*, which turns the skin into a mix of pus-leaking blackheads, zits, and cysts. One skin doctor (aka, dermatologist) thinks that this painful condition made Marx an angry and alienated man, and this led him to write about Communism in the first place! In 1867, Marx

wrote that his enemies "will remember my carbuncles until their dying day." *Yikes.*

UGLY MARKS VS. BEAUTY MARKS

Moles are sometimes called "beauty marks." I've always thought this was sort of cheap. Sure, if a mole is on a beautiful person it can be a beauty mark.[1] Otherwise it's just a mole!

No matter what your skin color is, you have a pigment in it called melanin. It's what gives your skin its color. (Albinos don't have melanin, but everyone else does.) Melanin is responsible for tanning any skin that gets exposed to sunlight. If melanin doesn't spread evenly in your skin but instead clusters in one spot, that's how you get a mole.

Moles are weird. Babies usually don't have any, but as people age, moles start cropping up. Some moles come and go pretty quickly, while others hang on for as long as forty years. And they come in ALL sizes. Their shapes can vary, too. Some moles stick out from the skin, while others are so flat, they are just like freckles.

The worst moles are the ones with hairs sticking out of them. *Urk!*

1. And it's *always* a woman. Who ever heard of a beauty mark on a man?

THICK-SKINNED?

Your skin may seem thin, but it's actually quite leathery. That's how ancient Aztec priests were able to make cloaks from the skin of people who'd been sacrificed to their gods. Speaking of skin removal, when Cardinal Lagrange of France died in 1402, the folks in charge of his body had a really gross job: they had to de-bone the Cardinal! The religious leader had insisted that his bones be buried at Avignon, but he wanted his skin and everything else left inside it to be buried at Amiens. (As you can guess, the Cardinal was not exactly a fun person. One of his tombs was inscribed, "Wretch, why are you so proud? You are nothing but ashes, and will, like me a fetid corpse, be food for worms.")

DANDRUFF

Since many skin cells only live for three days, dead skin is falling off you all the time. That's why bald people are lucky. Not only are we (oops, I mean "they") more intelligent than most people, but bald people also usually don't have dandruff problems. That's because hair is what keeps dead skin cells from falling away from the body, and especially the head. Instead, the dead cells get clustered together, and then they break off in big chunks of dandruff, or "seborrheic scruff," as the doctors call it.

Of course, you have dandruff falling off your whole body. About 80 percent of the dust in your house comes from dead skin cells, and if you saved all of your cells, you'd end up with about forty pounds of dead skin in your lifetime!

FUNGUS!

Do you ever jam your toes? Probably! Your feet are packed with more sweat glands then you can imagine, and they are constantly sweating. That means dirt, dead skin, and lint (from your socks) is going to gather in the wet spots between your toes. And there's your toe jam right there! (For fun, collect the lint from the dryer. Pull it apart and stuff it into a glass jar. Label it "Toe Jam" and put the jar in the refrigerator next to the jelly.)

Another problem your feet may run into is fungus. Most fungi like warm, wet places, and your feet probably qualify. Once you get some foot fungus, you'll notice an itching. This will be followed by scaly, raw skin, and sometimes blistering. By then you'll definitely want to do something about it!

This type of fungus can grow pretty much anywhere on your skin, but your feet and groin are the most likely spots. The worst part of foot fungus is when it gets underneath the toenail, which is, unfortunately, a GREAT hiding place. Once the fungus gets a toehold there (oh, snap!), it can take years to get rid of it.

OF COURSE, IF ALL THESE DISGUSTING FOOT PROB-LEMS ARE TOO MUCH FOR YOU, JUST GO BAREFOOT (OR WEAR SANDALS A LOT). AFTER ALL, THE ONLY REASON LINT AND FUNGUS HANG AROUND YOUR TOOTSIES IS BECAUSE YOU'RE CONSTANTLY ENCLOSING THEM IN LITTLE GREENHOUSES: SOCKS AND SHOES!

While you're staring at your feet (hey, how can you read this then?), you may see a callus someday. This is where the skin gets really thick, usually because of friction with a shoe. (Corns are sort of like mini-calluses.) Perhaps, like me, you have seen people grind away at their calluses with emery boards. This rubs bits of ground-up skin off the foot and into the air around the person who is grinding.

Keep away from these people!

BLISTERS

Some words are just perfect. I mean, the sound of the word perfectly matches its definition. *Blister* is like that; just looking at it makes me feel hot and, uh, blistery. You can get a blister if your skin gets rubbed too much (from yard work), or if your skin touches something really hot (from kitchen work), or even if you touch something really cold (from polar ice-cap work).

Do you know the difference between small blisters (*vesicles*) and big blisters (*bullae*)? Size! But no matter how big, the blisters will probably fill with a watery fluid that is mostly plasma. That's the stuff in your veins that your red blood cells float in. Plasma is actually sort of yellowish, but you don't notice it when you get cut because your red blood cells get all the attention.

Here's what's weird, though: a blister doesn't form UNDER your skin. Nope, it forms BETWEEN your skin! You see, your skin has layers. On the outside is the outer skin (epidermis), which is actually pretty much dead skin. It protects your inner skin (dermis), which is where your living skin cells are, along with blood vessels and nerves. And below both of these is the *subcutaneous* layer, which is where your skin's glands are. So when a blister fills with fluid, it's cushioning and protecting the dermis and subcutaneous layers from any damage.

And that's why you shouldn't pop a blister! If you wait to let the blister pop naturally, you'll give your skin time to repair itself.

WARTS AND ALL

There is a simple beauty to a wart. That's because you get warts by touching warts. So if you don't WANT a wart (and I'm guessing you don't), don't touch a wart!

Warts are spread by little skin viruses. And I think you already figured out where these skin viruses hang out: ON WARTS! If you're in a locker room and someone with warts on his feet is walking around barefoot and then you walk around barefoot behind him, you can get warts too!

Once one of the wart viruses lands on your skin, it tricks your skin cells into multiplying. That's all a wart is: too many skin cells. Stupid, huh? But once you have a wart, try not to touch it. It's usually best to just leave it alone. Most warts won't hang around forever. My theory is that they're just playing a little joke on you and your skin, and once the joke doesn't seem funny anymore, the wart moves on!

SCABIES: A COMBINATION OF SCABS AND RABIES?

You just know that anything that rhymes with "rabies" is going to be bad, right? Scabies is a skin disease involving itching and red spots. It's caused by insects called "itch mites." I told you it was bad!

These mites like to tunnel under a person's skin (especially between their fingers) and hang out, lay eggs, and basically make trouble. When the eggs hatch, little larval itch mites (like tiny caterpillars) grow up and are quite happy to jump onto new people to continue this cycle. To stop them from doing this, the infected person has to commit larvicide.[2]

B.O. AND OTHER STINKS

For two long years, Swiss researchers sweated it out over a problem that has continually haunted mankind:

DO MEN AND WOMEN HAVE THE SAME B.O.?

The answer is no. It turns out that men's armpits usually smell like gouda cheese. Women's underarms smell like onions. And if you think you like the smell of cheese more

2.   The killing of larvae.

than onions, you'd better like it a LOT more, because men sweat about 40 percent more than women.

A lot of a person's body odor comes from sweat. Since humans come equipped with about two million sweat glands, there's a whole lot of stinking going on. If you could harvest pure sweat, it wouldn't be a clear fluid. Nope, it'd look sort of like watered-down milk! And even if all you do is just sit around, you'll still sweat just over a pint of this "milk" every day. Some of the things in your sweat are water, salt, and a waste protein called urea. All of these are also found in your pee!

Of course, humans use deodorants to mask their cheese and onion smells. But not so fast! It turns out that when a man puts on deodorant, he is only able to mask his B.O. from other men. That's because women have the ability to detect a person's underarm odor beneath his or her deodorant. It's true! So remember to take a quick shower if you reek. And if you still stink, reach for one of these words to describe your aroma: *fetid, nauseating, rancid, revolting, sickening, stink-tacular,* or *vile.*

"WAITER, MY SOUP SMELLS LIKE SWEAT!"

French onion soup comes with melted cheese on top. It's sweaty-licious!

THE GROSSEST SPORT OF ALL

You probably think of your own sweat as somewhat gross. And as for other people's sweat, *puh-leeze*. So, thinking about sweat, what do you think is the grossest sport of all? If you ever run in a marathon, the people running around you are practically *spraying* sweat out of their bodies. And in wrestling, two sweaty people rub their B.O. all over each other.

But I think hockey takes the prize for Stinkiest Sport. Hockey players wear a lot of padded equipment, and then they race around the rink in it. And once that B.O. smell gets in the pads, it's not coming back out! Hockey gloves smell so bad that players who want to be jerks give their opponents a "face wash." This is done by pushing a stinky glove into another player's face!

YOUR NOSE: AN OWNER'S MANUAL

Right now, you might be trying to remember a time when you smelled a person's B.O. Was it cheesy or oniony? But restrain any impulse you have to smell the *osmidrosis* in someone's armpit right now. I give this warning because some people like to test out just how horrible a bad smell can be.

This behavior has been around for a long time. In 1558, a man named Giovanni della Casa begged his fellow Italians to stop pointing out disgusting things for others to smell. He wrote that a person should *not* ask, "I should like to know how much that stinks," when it would be much more proper and polite to say, "Because it stinks, I will not smell it."

But how do we know if something even stinks in the first place? Here's how it works: molecules of the stinky stuff

break off and hover in the air. Imagine a molecule of cheesy B.O. breaking off from someone's armpit. Let's say this B.O. molecule travels up some lucky human's nostril (*woo hoo!*). Up, up, and way up into the nose it goes, until it eventually comes to a patch of dark yellow skin covered with a little mucus. This is where the smell receptors (called dendrites) are. The B.O. molecule lands on the mucus and goes through it. Then the *dendrites* (which are tiny and sort of hairy-looking) sense the molecule. The dendrites get a "reading" of it and send a message to your brain: *cheesy!*

Besides your underarms, the heaviest concentration of sweat glands is in your crotch. That's TWO bad smells combining for evil! Luckily, Japanese scientists have come up with cutting-edge underwear (ouch!) that can deal with this problem. Named "J-ware," these undies are designed to dry quickly and kill bacteria. And since bacteria are the culprits for making things stink, these are stink-free underwear! Miracle of miracles!

THE GREATEST STINK OF ALL

Kailash Singh of India has not washed for thirty-five years! He made a promise not to bathe until all the problems confronting his country end. So it might be a while before he breaks out the bubble bath.

SNOT AND BOOGERS

The ancient Greek named Hippocrates is honored today as the "Father of Medicine." Wow! I'd be happy just to be known as the "Cousin of Cough Syrup." As a measure of the great influence of Hippocrates, today's doctors must make a promise called the "Hippocratic oath." (This includes the famous line "First, do no harm …")

So how wise was Hippocrates? Well, he believed that one of the main functions of the brain was to make snot.

WHAT? BRAIN SNOT?! WHAT A NINCOMPOOP! SOME FATHER OF MEDICINE HIPPOCRATES TURNED OUT TO BE!

Brain snot aside, I can't make up my mind about which one of these words I like best: *mucus, snot, phlegm,* or *sputum.* They're all so awesome! But there are slight differences between them:

MUCUS: This thick, gooey stuff is in your nose and throat. And it's also inside your digestive system, lungs, and urinary tract. Its job is to coat, soothe, and protect—like Pepto Bismol! Mucus also does a great job of trapping all the dust and nasty junk that you breathe in every day.

NASAL MONUMENT

The Mimizuka is a Japanese war monument dedicated to the country's battle with Korea in the late 1500s, in which samurai warriors enshrined the noses and ears of over thirty thousand Korean soldiers. (These were easier to transport back to Japan than the usual samurai warrior prize: the whole head.)

SNOT: This word applies strictly to the mucus that lines your sinuses.

PHLEGM: This word is generally used for the mucus that you clear out of your throat. You might cough up or swallow phlegm, but you wouldn't blow it out your schnozz.

SPUTUM: Once you've coughed up your phlegm and spat it out, *voilà!* It's called sputum. You can also call it a loogie if you want.

I know what you're thinking: "But what about boogers?" Okay, here's the recipe for boogers. The inside of your nose is coated with moisture, a bit of salt, and a dash of a sticky protein called mucin. Together, these form the mucus that traps nasty things like dust and germs that you breathe. It's better to trap that junk in your nose than to allow it into your lungs.

After the mucus in your nose traps enough of this stuff, it will dry up and turn into a booger. But be sure to let your boogers ripen, for Pete's sake! If your mucus never dries but instead remains in its liquid "snot" stage, you have two choices: you can blow it out or swallow it. I know, that sounds harsh. But I had to prepare you for the following heart-rending story.

A HEART-RENDING STORY

Like any first-grade kid, I did plenty of snuffling and swallowing when I had a cold. But I almost had a heart attack when a friend of mine named Brian gave a big snort and then showed me a bunch of green loogies … in his mouth. How did those get there? When I realized the horrible truth (I've been swallowing snot?!), I went to great lengths to blow my nose for minutes afterward.

What's weird is that I'd never really understood that if my mouth opened to my throat, and my nose opened to my throat, then my mouth and my nose were connected! This relationship was confirmed when I was riding my bike

WHO WANTS TO MAKE SNOT?

Need to make some snot? (Not from your nose, that is?) Here's how:

Get some Cheese Whiz. Add a dash of green food coloring to it. Experiment until you get the color right. And you're done! This green cheesy substance is ideal for dipping chips. Or hide some in a handkerchief and pretend to sneeze or blow your nose into it. Fun for the whole family!

219

PICK YOUR STYLE!

BRAIN STABBING: This is when you burrow so deeply for a booger, you jab your frontal lobe.

THE BLESSING OF PRIVACY: Looks like no one is around! Time to do some finger-stretching exercises and dig in. (And just when you're making progress, you find that someone's been watching you all along!)

THE CURSE OF RHINORRHEA: You try and try, but your nose is so runny, you can't get any traction.

NASAL DECEPTION: Upon initial exploration, the booger seems solid and ready for harvest. But once it's removed, the booger is actually long, slimy, and impossible to get rid of! Get me a hanky, stat!

I'M INNOCENT, I TELL YA!: You were *not* picking your nose. It had to be a weird optical illusion that made it *look* like you were! If you find yourself unjustly accused, ask the prosecution to present its evidence. (Y'know, the actual booger.)

THE ATTEMPT TO CAPITALIZE ON THE CURSE OF INNOCENCE: Nothing to see here! I'm just stretching my arms ... yep, I might scratch my nose for a moment ... well, if nobody is watching, I might just check my inventory ... got one!

GETTING LUCKY: You just absentmindedly swiped your nose and dislodged a booger behemoth. Score!

yesterday. I was breathing hard through my mouth and nose. Suddenly, a large black flying bug swooped toward my face and got too close to my nostrils as I was breathing in.

I snorted that big bug right up my nose! But he was moving so fast, he flew through my sinuses in no time, and the next thing I knew he was in my throat. I gave a cough, and out came the bug. The poor little guy must have been covered in booger juice and spit. But somehow he reached down deep and flew bravely off into the sunset.

But for a moment, I bet his whole life flashed before my nostril.

KEEP YOUR FINGERS OUT OF IT

Let me share some of the interesting studies that have been done on mucus. For example, a scientist studying nose-picking wrote: "This first population survey of nose-picking suggests that it is an almost universal practice in adults."

What's amazing to me isn't that kids pick their noses, but that apparently all adults do too! And I'd always thought that this was a joke:

QUESTION: What do you find inside a clean nose?
ANSWER: Fingerprints.

While nose-picking is universal, there is a segment of our population that does something society really frowns upon. Apparently, three out of every hundred nose-pickers picks a winner and then eats it. This means that 3 percent of everyone you know eats boogers.

I've been looking up my own nostrils as research, and there are actual hairs up there! This makes me sad because ever since I was younger (like, yesterday), I've mocked men who have visible hair in their nose. Sometimes this nose hair is so long and beefy, it hangs out of the nostrils. Worst of all is when it grows out of the nostrils and then merges with the man's moustache!

Anyway, these big nose hairs are called *vibrissae*. Like the rest of your nostrils, they get coated with mucus. This allows the vibrissae to help catch passing bits of pollution, dust, and grit. So while a man with thick nose hair is disgusting, his upper sinuses actually contain fewer boogers than the rest of ours do!

There are other much smaller hairs that go live farther up your nostrils. These are called *cilia*, and they actually move back and forth on their own.

YES, YOU HAVE MOVING HAIRS IN YOUR NOSE. CONGRATULATIONS!

This movement by the cilia works your mucus to the back of your throat at a speed of an inch every four minutes. When the mucus eventually gets to the back of your throat, you either swallow it or hack it up! There are cilia in your lungs doing the same thing, but down there, the little hairs move irritants UP to your throat so you can get rid of them.

Things that stop your cilia from working include:

★ INFECTION! If your sinuses clog up due to infection, the mucus can't be moved out to your throat, and your cilia give up trying. Allergies can also cause this. Result: Mucus drips down from the back of the nose, causing you to wipe your nostrils a lot. (This is called post-nasal drip.)

★ TEMPERATURE CHANGES! Going from warm air to cold air will temporarily freeze up your cilia. Result: Clear mucus will run from your nostrils.

★ BRAIN SNOT! I've been reading Hippocrates' notes, and he says that if a person has a headache, the brain will not be able to make mucus properly. Result: Brain snot? What an idiot!

If your cilia detect something in your nose that doesn't belong there, like a germ, a pea, or some pepper, they will go on green alert. This will result in a *sternutation*.[3]

3.   A sneeze.

I HOPE YOU HAD A TISSUE.

Well, I guess that's it. Oh wait, I have something REALLY important to tell you. Remember how I couldn't make up my mind on what word to use?

I prefer *phlegm.* Now go in peace.

Food, Drink, and Other Harmless Hazards

Some of the things you eat are truly disgusting. But hey, it's not your fault. How were you supposed to know you've been eating cigarette butts?

Don't feel bad. Heck, I've been chowing down on maggots for years. What choice do I have? I like food. And almost all packaged foods contain *something* nasty. For example, a can of mushrooms is legally allowed to contain twenty maggots for every hundred grams of mushrooms. It's the law! In the United States, the Food and Drug Administration (FDA) legally defines maggots as "harmless hazards."

"How can a hazard be harmless?" you ask. "That's like healthy poison!" Oh, it's all written up in a booklet called *The Food Defect Action Levels*. This booklet is a double whammy: it's really boring *and* really gross. If you muck your way through it, you'll learn that all of the following items are "harmless hazards":

★ insects and their eggs
★ insect filth (excrement)
★ insect larvae (maggots!)
★ mammal poop (usually rat poop)
★ mold
★ mildew
★ parasites
★ rodent filth and hair

Maybe worst of all is the category called "foreign matter." It's made up of "sticks, stones, burlap bagging, cigarette butts, etc." Sticks and stones? Those can break your bones! (And what about your small intestine?) In addition to "foreign matter," foods like hot dogs can have the ground-up snout, ear, stomach, or esophagus (the "food tube") of a pig in them. But you won't find these items listed on the label of ingredients. Instead you'll see "with by-products" or "with variety meats." When it comes to "variety meats," you can count me out!

★ RYPHOPHAGY: **To eat something disgusting.**

What this all means is that, on average, you eat two pounds of mites, flies, and maggots every year. That is totally gross. It's also almost totally harmless, because it turns out that these items really won't hurt you in the small amounts that they occur.

It's apparently impossible to keep flies and rats out of our food. As the FDA says, it's "impractical to grow, harvest, or process raw products that are totally free of non-hazardous, naturally occurring, unavoidable defects." *Rats!* That is to say, we can't keep rats and flies away from our food. Okay, okay. (But about those cigarette butts?)

WHAT'S FOR DESSERT?

The Web site www.candyaddict.com lists the ten most disgusting candies ever made. Some of these sickening sweets include Hose Nose (a slimy candy picked from a plastic nose), Sour Flush (sort of like Pixy Stix in a little toilet), Chocka Ca-Ca (talk about overkill!), earwax candy (it comes in a fake ear), and Candy Scabs (fake Band-Aids with fake scabs).

Actually, you know what? I'm full.

DIRT

You may doubt me, but eating dirt is safer than eating many foods.

I'm not saying that dirt is good for you. But some doctors are! Since ancient times, cultures from Africa to Greece to North America have eaten certain clays for medicinal reasons. How could this be? Well, your body needs substances like iron, manganese, and calcium, and these can be found in certain kinds of dirt. Further, the dirt found in termite mounds has kaolinite in it, which prevents diarrhea. In southern Africa, people with tummy troubles have dined on termite dirt with good success!

So maybe parents shouldn't freak out when Junior starts eating dirt. Because along with the dirt (which can't be digested anyway) there are millions of bacteria. And some scientists are starting to think that these bacteria can help build a strong immune system.

After all, there are already about ninety trillion microbes living inside you. And many of them are what help keep you healthy! Because of this, some doctors advise not worrying about eating a little dirt. They point out that farm kids play in the dirt a lot and hang around lots of animals. And compared to city kids, they are much less likely to get allergies and certain diseases!

THE DEMON CHEESE!

Of course, the problem with dirt is that it tastes like, well, *dirt*, so let's try talking about a more delicious food: cheese!

Cheeses can range from being so soft they're almost soupy to being so hard you could get knocked cold by one if a strange person attacked you with … a hard cheese. But *all* cheeses probably got their start thousands of years ago from an unknown Arab who was riding a horse or camel under the desert sun. As the Arab traveled, the pouch of milk he'd brought for his trip bounced along in the heat. When our rider stopped for a break, he was not amused to find his pouch full of curdled cheese. *Dang it!*

But he was brave or desperate enough to try some, and the next thing you know, everyone was leaving out milk to curdle, harden, putrefy, and decay. Yep, that's how you make cheese!

Theoretically, you can make cheese from any mammal that produces thick milk. So there are cheeses made from cows, sheep, goats, and even reindeer. (I'll bet whale cheese would work pretty well, too.) You may wonder why there aren't any cheeses that come from omnivores or carnivores. Think about it: Who's going to milk a grizzly bear?!

As for human milk, it's apparently too watery to make good cheese. That's probably just as well. I don't know if I could handle a slice of human cheese on my avocado sandwich. Plus, would eating human cheese be cannibalism? (I guess not, since babies drink the milk all the time … but still!)

Besides, think of the crazy variety of cheeses already available. Even if you look at just the stinky cheeses, there are hundreds of different types. Of course, all cheeses are somewhat smelly; that's what happens when you let milk go bad. But that's not the only reason some cheese stinks. If you've ever seen Roquefort cheese, you know it has blue ribbons of color in it. These colored bits give the cheese a tangy taste. And those ribbons are actually mold—as in FUNGUS.

The world's stinkiest cheese is apparently named Vieux Boulogne. This soft French cheese beat out more than a dozen others in a competition that featured nineteen human stink testers as well as an "electronic nose" programmed to analyze cheese aromas.

How stinky is this cheese? Well, a cheese named Époisses de Bourgogne smells so bad, it's been outlawed on all public transportation in France. And Vieux Boulogne beat it! But I think the contest was rigged, because it left out a cheese so deadly, it's technically illegal everywhere. I refer to Casu Marzu, the demon cheese!

Casu Marzu is made on the Italian island of Sardinia. Its name translates to "rotten cheese," and it is also nicknamed "maggot cheese." That's because you can't make it properly without flies laying eggs in it! The maggots supposedly enhance the cheese's flavor by eating it and excreting cheese poop, which makes the Casu Marzu putrefy and ferment.

When bringing a piece of Casu Marzu to your mouth, you're supposed to cover it with one hand so that maggots don't jump in your face. Yep, the cheese is alive! Too scared to do that? Then just cut a piece and tie if off in a plastic bag. When the bag stops squirming, the maggots are dead and it's safe to eat. (Yes, this is how it's done.) People who eat it say that Casu Marzu has a "gluey" texture, but between the squirming maggots and the burning sensation in your mouth and nostrils, you don't mind it that much.

Public health officials have banned Casu Marzu everywhere, but you know how that goes: when you outlaw a rotten cheese, then, uh, only outlaws will have rotten cheese. And if you can't get your hands on some Casu Marzu, you can always travel to Germany to sample its Milbenkäse.

This reddish-brown cheese swarms with cheese mites for three months to a year before it's brought out to eat.

PLANTS

Plants just can't compete with animals when it comes to being gross. Sure, you may THINK broccoli is gross, but try eating a tarantula, and then we'll talk. So all I want to say about gross plants is this: there are people who pretend the rhubarb plant is good, even delicious.

THESE PEOPLE ARE VERY WRONG.

If you aren't familiar with rhubarb, it's a plant with thick stalks and broad leaves. But if you eat the leaves or roots of the rhubarb, you get poisoned by the oxalic acid in them. If you eat the stalks, you find that they're really tough and acidy tasting. But if you cook the heck out of the stalks and put them in a pie with mounds of sugar, the rhubarb is barely edible (and still tart).

Put it this way: the ancient Greeks called rhubarb the "vegetable of barbarians." They were on to something!

Elsewhere in the plant kingdom, there are certain seaweeds that are quite slimy. And there is also an algae that looks like wet, used toilet paper. It's nickname is "rock snot." *Blech!* And, of course, no discussion of disgusting plants is complete without mentioning the large and dangerously spiked Southeast Asian fruit called durian. This fruit smells bad. Really bad. Anthony Bourdain described it this way: "It smelled like you'd buried somebody holding a big wheel of Stilton [cheese] in his arms, then dug him up a few weeks later."

POP QUIZ!

Match the gross-sounding food with its definition! (Answers below.)

1. Bladderwrack
2. Spotted Dick
3. Skum saus
4. Wheat germ
5. Bloater
6. Scrunchion
7. Wiener Krapfen
8. Toad-in-the-hole
9. Bratklops
10. Chlodnik

a. Pork cut into cubes and fried
b. English pudding
c. Germs are good for you!
d. A scummy sauce from Norway
e. Dried fish
f. An Austrian doughnut
g. A fried egg in a piece of toast
h. Edible seaweed
i. A cold Polish soup
j. German fried meatballs

(Answers: 1. h 2. b 3. d 4. c 5. e 6. a 7. f 8. g 9. j 10. i

The durian stinks so much, it is illegal to have in Singapore. If you break open the twelve-pound fruit and survive the aroma, you're ready to eat its pudding-like pulp. And apparently it tastes pretty good! But the horrible smell means that eating the durian is like what one person called "eating ice cream in an outhouse."

GOOD EATING IN THE ROCKY MOUNTAINS

Cheese and seaweed aside, there are plenty of other gross foods that people eat on purpose. So let's continue our discussion with a look at oysters without shells. This cowboy delicacy is known as Rocky Mountain Oysters, cowboy caviar, swinging sirloin, and lamb or calf fries, but whatever you call them, they do NOT taste like chicken. (Or oysters!)

YES, I'M REFERRING TO TESTICLES.

Sorry, but there was no other way to write that. As you probably know, male pigs, lambs, and calves usually get gelded at an early age. "Gelded" means the same thing as neutered, fixed, or castrated. And that means that someone cuts their testicles off. Why do something so horrible to an innocent animal? It supposedly makes the animal's meat more appetizing.

Okay, but what happens to a gelded animal's testicles? Some of them find their way to the kitchen. This custom was imported by Basques into the western United States in the late 1800s. (Basques hail from a territory between France and Spain.) The Basques were not shy about castration; if a knife were not around, they would obtain the testicles using their teeth. (Really.) Of course, the testicles were cooked, and today, the classic recipe is to dip them in cornmeal and fry them.

There are plenty of cultures that eat animal testicles. And in almost every case, it's men who want to eat animal testicles because these men think this will make them feel more "manly." Of course, this is idiotic. The idea that eating an animal's private parts would make a man more manly is as logical as thinking that eating a hairy animal would help a bald man grow hair!

DRINK

O kay, maybe you're getting a little dehydrated and you'd like to take a beverage break. Fair enough. How about some coffee? After all, there's nothing gross about coffee (except its taste!). Unless you're enjoying a hot cup of kopi luwak, that is.

Here's how it works. If you look up in a coffee tree growing in parts of Southeast Asia and Indonesia, you might see an animal known as the common palm civet, or luwak. (The luwak is a cat that looks like a weasel and is actually a marsupial, but never mind that now.) This interesting animal eats the ripest coffee beans. Coffee beans actually have a fruity outer covering, and while the luwak digests this, the coffee bean itself passes entirely through the animal's digestive system, and it shows up again in its poop.

Now it gets weird. Humans then go around and collect the luwak poop, separating the beans out and roasting them to sell for a VERY high price. What's so special about luwak-poop coffee? Apparently, the enzymes in the luwak's stomach give the coffee beans a special flavor. The flavor of luwak poop coffee is so good, it retails from $120 to $600 a pound! (You can get it cheaper in Indonesia. But wherever you drink it, it's good to the last dropping.)

I guess the grossest thing that humans drink is blood. Animal blood has shown up in a number of recipes through-out history, many of which are still around. For instance, in Scandinavia, people still enjoy the time-honored recipe of *svartsoppa*, a soup made with goose blood. And in Vietnam, it's a big deal to go to a restaurant and have a live cobra brought to your table. The snake's heart is cut out right there and placed into a cup, still pumping blood. The diner then throws the cup back and swallows. The heart and

I KNEW THAT TASTED FUNNY!

British Admiral Horatio Nelson died in 1805 off the Spanish coast. To keep his body preserved for the trip home, sailors put it into a barrel full of brandy. Mistake! Sailors love brandy, and it turned out that they were secretly siphoning off the drink during the homeward trip. By the time the admiral got home, the barrel was nearly empty.

GERMANS LOVE MEAT!

In German, the phrase "Wie eine Made im Speck leben" means that someone is "living a life of luxury." But translated literally, it means, "to live like a maggot in bacon."

cobra blood go down the hatch, and as it goes, the heart's still beating: *ba-bump, ba-bump … Blech!*

As your scabs have taught you, liquid blood will turn into a solid. And so there are a number of dishes using blood as a solid or semi-solid ingredient. In Portugal, animal blood is simmered until it turns into sort of a scabby cake. Then it's thrown into soup or stew as flavoring! In the United Kingdom, there's blood pudding, and in Germany, you can slice up some *blutwurst* (blood sausage). Many of these recipes combine blood with lots of fat. For example, one *blutwurst* recipe combines pig blood with chopped pig's lung and diced bacon. If you eat it, the blood sausage will clog your arteries.

Call it the pig's revenge!

EATING MEAT

Humans will eat any animal that isn't poisonous. And some that are! The skin and guts of the blowfish (aka, puffer fish or fugu) has a deadly poison inside it that's 150,000 times more powerful than strychnine. If this poison is eaten, the victim dies a horrible death.

SO, OF COURSE, PEOPLE EAT IT!

In Japan, blowfish is considered a great delicacy. Trained chefs carefully remove the poisonous parts of the fish, and then diners dig in. Of course, sometimes the chefs make mistakes, and every year, dozens of people eat blowfish and feel their lips start to get numb. Then they die.

You'd think that, with all the reasons NOT to eat blowfish, at least it would be delicious. You'd think wrong. Apparently it's a bland fish that tastes almost like any other fish.

MAN, PEOPLE ARE SO WEIRD!

As for eating non-toxic meat, humans play a lot of mind games there too. Most people won't eat pure animal fat or drink animal blood. But if you take "meat juice" (blood) and mix it with melted fat, that's how you make gravy! And I'm guessing you've had that before.

Another mind game we play is pretending there is some huge difference between eating, say, a dog and a pig. But it's just a game of "pretend." Don't get me wrong, it's strange for me to imagine people eating animals that I've always thought of as pets. But in places like Korea and Southeast Asia, dogs are being eaten right now. At the same time, more than a billion Jews and Muslims are going out of their way to avoid eating pigs.

Whether a pig or dog is eaten has less to do with the animal and more to do with human attitudes. For example, I was ordering take-out Chinese food for a group of people, and I asked if anyone would eat frogs' legs.

"NOOO!" THE ENTIRE GROUP CRIED OUT.

"I'M NOT EATING AN AMPHIBIAN!" PROTESTED ONE WOMAN.

"FROGS LIVE IN SWAMPS," SAID ANOTHER.

"AND THEY'RE SLIPPERY!" I YELLED. (I WAS CARRIED AWAY BY THE PROTEST.)

The group then asked me to order beef, seafood, pork, and chicken. And I secretly ordered the frogs' legs just to see what would happen. After getting the food, I put all the different containers out on a table, with the frogs' legs in the middle of the pack.

By the end of the meal, the frogs' legs were all gone! People thought they were chicken wings, and they LOVED them. Finally, I couldn't stand it anymore. "Those were frogs' legs!" I trumpeted. I foolishly believed everyone would be pleased to learn that it was silly to pretend one animal was better or worse to eat than another.

But nobody thought it was funny. Nobody changed their attitude about the way they thought about meat. And nobody let me order Chinese take-out ever again!

Horses are another example of an animal that people have certain beliefs about eating. Some people ride them. Some people drink and ride them. When Marco Polo visited Mongolia, he observed Mongol horse-riders drinking blood right from the necks of their horses! The horse-riders

NO JELLY FOR ME

Among Inuit tribes, there is a legendary recipe for Moose Nose Jelly. It involves cooking and re-cooking the nose of a moose until it turns to jelly. (I guess you could see that coming.)

would just drain off a small amount for nutrition. If necessary, they would even stitch up the horse's neck again.

As for eating horses, it's been legal in France since 1811, and horse meat is also eaten raw in Belgium, Sweden, and Japan. (They say that colts are best because they're tender.) If you find the idea of eating a horse disgusting, let me ask: Would you eat a zebra? What about an antelope? A deer? A sheep? See what I mean? It's all a game of pretend. If you think it's disgusting to eat a horse, it's really just as disgusting to eat ANY mammal.

In Peru, guinea pigs get cooked up every year by the tens of millions. But they reproduce so fast, there's no danger of their going extinct. And there is probably a culture out there somewhere that eats hamsters, but I don't have the heart to look in to that right now.[1]

Maybe part of what freaks us out isn't the KIND of animal being eaten, but the PART of the animal that's being eaten. Perhaps no domesticated animal can rival the sheep for how long humans have been eating it. If you go to the Iranian city of Tehran, you'll find restaurants specializing in a breakfast soup named *kaleh pache,* which translates to "heads and hooves." It's seasoned with lemon and cinnamon and made with a sheep's entire head (including tongue, eyes, and brain) and its hooves.

Who came up with the bright idea of combining these things? I don't know! But based on reports, the eye of a sheep tastes oily. It can be plucked right out of the sheep's skull. As for the sheep's tongue, it tastes powdery. (How nasty is it to taste an animal's taste buds? *Ick!*) There are also the sheep's lips, gums, and snout, all ready for a hearty breakfast-eater.

I know I'm supposed to be grossing you out, but I suppose it shows a certain respect for an animal when its entire body is eaten and not wasted. Take pigs in Portugal. After being butchered, nearly every single part of the pig finds a home (usually in someone's stomach). "But what about the pig's

---

1.   Dang it, I couldn't resist. It turns out that humans have been eating hamsters and gerbils (!) for thousands of years. Apparently, those little plastic hamster balls aren't much of a defense against a hungry caveman.

urinary bladder? Surely no one wants that!" you say.

Wrong! In northern Portugal, the pig's bladder is inflated, tied off, and given to the kids. Then they use it for a soccer ball. *Goal!*

BIRDS

Eating bird embryos is sort of nasty if you think about it. But people cook up chicken eggs so much, we sort of forget that's what we're doing. But what if you took a fertilized chicken egg and let it mature a little more? Would people still eat it?

Yep! Names like *balut* and *hot vin lon* are what these chicken or duck eggs are called. The baby fowl has developed to the point that it has a head, wings, veins, and feathers. So, yeah, it's an almost-ready-to-hatch embryo until a person pops open the shell and pours the contents into his or her mouth. The embryo is apparently crunchy. (Maybe those crunches will drown out the sounds of my screaming.)

To distract myself from these horrors, I'll tell you that kiwi birds lay some pretty amazing eggs. Kiwis are small black birds found only in New Zealand, but even though they're small, they lay some of the biggest eggs in the world. A five-pound kiwi can lay a one-pound egg! That's sort of like a hundred-pound kid busting a grumpy that weighs twenty pounds.

While kiwis are pretty uncommon, you've definitely seen pigeons before. Some people find these common city birds disgusting, but pigeons are very popular food birds. They're usually called "squab," and they come in a variety of colors. A squab weighs about one pound, which makes the bird ideal for a single-person meal.

Birds can taste a lot like whatever they eat, and so city pigeons aren't nearly as good as squabs fed yummier diets than, say, trash.

Since doves are smaller than pigeons, and since they're the symbol of peace, you'd think people would leave them alone. No such luck; the birds still end up on dinner plates world-wide. There are a lot of unlikely birds that get eaten. The ancient Romans used to dine on flamingos, and even para-keets and parrots are not safe from hungry humans.

INVERTEBRATES

While I like to think I have an open mind, I can't understand how humans started eating an animal that leaves a trail of slime behind it. Sure, snails are easy to catch, but so are rocks, and we don't eat those!

The ancient Romans grilled snails in oil, and people today dip their *escargots* in hot butter. What's odd is that while snails get eaten by the millions, slugs get left alone. I have no idea why this is. Are slugs a little too naked to be popping into one's mouth? Because there's not much of a difference between the two!

HOW TO EAT FRIED WORMS

INGREDIENTS
mealworms or earthworms
olive oil
bread crumbs

SUPPLIES
colander
paper towels or wax
paper on a plate
frying pan

Mealworms are eaten in
many cultures. I can't think of any right now, but take my word
for it. What you want to do is get some live mealworms. Check
your phone book, look on the Internet, or go to a big pet shop;
they usually have them there. (If you're using earthworms for
this recipe, just start digging for them.)

To prepare your worms, put them into a colander and rinse
them off. Make sure that you get all the gunk off them; you
just want to eat the worm. (Right?) Lay the worms out on some
paper towels (to dry them out) or wax paper. They may be
squirming a bit, so shove them into the fridge to chill them out.

While the worms are chilling, pour enough olive oil into the
frying pan to cover the bottom. Then break up a couple of pieces
of bread into breadcrumbs and you're almost ready. Get the
frying pan hot and get the worms out of the fridge. They should
be "knocked out" enough at this point that they won't feel you
roll them in the breadcrumbs and then put them into the frying
pan. You want to stir-fry the worms in the oil until they are
crispy, then take them out of the pan, let them cool, and enjoy!

But while land slugs don't get eaten much, sea slugs (which can weigh two pounds!) do have their fans. If you'd like to eat one, just capture a sea slug and boil it for two days. It'll still be as crunchy as a bamboo shoot, but at least you'll be able to swallow it down!

If having a sea slug work its way through your guts isn't your idea of a good time, consider eating another invertebrate of the sea. For some reason, I've always been suspicious of shellfish. Maybe it's because my parents used to take the family "clamming." We'd wade out in the surf and plunge our hands deep into the sand to pull up razorback clams. (After cutting my hand a few times, I realized where the name came from.)

After filling pail after pail, we kids would try to warm our shivering, cut bodies while the clams were prepared. Then, mealtime! I'll never forget the horrible disappointment I had the first time I ate a clam. First, it looks disgusting. Second, it tastes exactly like Gristle of the Sea.

"And tomorrow we can have clam chowder!" my mom enthused. *Mmmm!* Chunks of gristle in milk! If the chowder is too hot, you can blow on it. And if you eat more than a small bowl of the stuff, you will blow chowder.

Humans eat plenty of other shellfish, but I think they only do it on bets and double dares. Why eat abalone? After you pound on it for a few days with a giant wooden hammer, it'll taste just like a baseball mitt. Oysters? I don't eat any animal that changes from female to male to female and then back again every year! (They do that, you know.)

To get out of eating shellfish, I'm even willing to cook up the animal that Socrates called the "intestines of the soil": earthworms!

Insects like grasshoppers, ants, and termites are commonly eaten. (If you think these might be too small to eat, an African queen termite is the size of a potato!) And beetles like giant water bugs and cockroaches are totally edible. It turns out that almost every beetle on the planet can be eaten by humans. But if you think I'm putting a dung beetle in my mouth, there are two problems: the dung and the beetle!

A Bogong moth is a huge Australian moth that migrates in the spring. Aborigines sometimes roast and mash the moths to make something called "moth meat," which is said to have a nutty taste.

If a Bogong moth gets caught in a web, it can lead us to our next dinner guest: the spider. *All* spiders are venomous meat-eaters. Yet you'll find people happily dining on arachnids from tarantulas to, uh, other spiders all over the tropics. Has the heat driven these people insane?

IN A WORD, YES!

A tarantula can be barbecued or roasted on the coals of a fire in a large leaf. After it's cooked, you apparently just sort of break through the skin and pull the meat out like you would for a crab. Those in the know say it tastes like shrimp, not chicken. Of course, these are the same people who are using the tarantula's fangs for toothpicks. (Like I said, they're insane.)

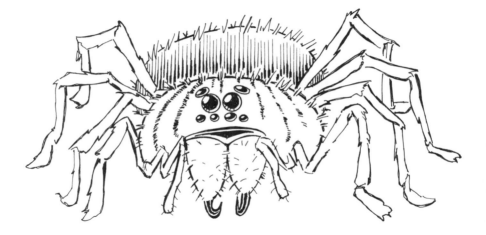

MEAT GARDENS

This idea is *sooo* weird. There are science labs that can "grow" meat in test tubes. This offers a way to eat meat without killing an animal! The idea is that people could grow their own meat at home. Also called "engineered meat," it can be designed to taste like beef or pork ... or anything else! According to Toronto's *Globe and*

Mail, before a person goes to bed, he/she would "throw starter cells and a package of growth medium into the (coffeemaker–size) meat maker and wake up to harvest-fresh sausage for breakfast."

I just told someone about this, and he said, "Meat from a meat-maker? Gross!" (But how is getting meat the "old-fashioned way" any less gross?)

IT TAKES GUTS

I'm pretty sure that for every organ inside a pig or cow, there's a human somewhere who will eat it. Lung? Stomach? Pancreas? Bring it on!

Maybe the most common way to eat animal guts is in sausage. Sausages are mostly made up of ground meats. And what keeps the ground meat from falling apart is the skin wrapped around the sausage. This skin is usually a pig, cow, or sheep intestine. Pretty weird, huh? Poop used to go through that animal intestine, and now the animal's intestine goes though your intestine! Of course, there is a substitute sausage skin that's made from a digestible plastic. But I'm not sure that's any less gross!

Since we're talking about people eating meat, I think we can agree that animals should be cared for thoughtfully

LET'S FIND OUT MORE!

Learn about sweetmeats. How sweet are they? Keep a trash can nearby in case you get sickened by where sweetmeats come from.

and slaughtered in a quick, humane way. And that's why *foie gras* has been outlawed in some parts of the world. It's a paste made from the swollen livers of ducks or geese. But to get the livers tasting the "right" way, a *foie gras* rancher grabs a duck and shoves a funnel down its throat. This funnel goes all the way to the animal's stomach. Then the animal is force-fed (or force-gorged) to digest more food than it would ever eat naturally.

This process is so disgusting, food celebrity Anthony Bourdain almost blew chunks when he watched a French duck being fed like this. And after eating *foie gras* and taking a car ride home, he DID throw up. Spectacularly!

As bad as it is, I think *foie gras* might be tied for grossness with Scotland's *haggis*. The poet Robert Burns described this dish as "gushing entrails"—and he was trying to be nice! To make it, get a sheep's stomach and fill it with oatmeal, fat, and a sheep's cut-up liver, esophagus, heart, lungs, and brain. Then let it simmer for four hours, and pour Scotch whiskey over the whole thing. But this is *not* take-out food: a shipment of *haggis* was once not allowed into the United States because it was considered "unfit" for humans to eat!

PEE PIES AND POOP

Hey, I just realized something: your kidneys (p. 45) filter your pee. This means they are constantly filled with urine. So why, oh why, do people eat kidneys? There are even kidney pies that are considered delicacies! I don't know about you, but any pie that smells like pee is not for me. (Alexandre Dumas—author of *The Three Musketeers*—even wrote a famous French cookbook in which he stated that kidneys are best when they still have a whiff of urine about them!)

As for poop, humans generally avoid eating it. (Thank goodness!) But there have been exceptions. (*Dang it!*) Native Americans of the American Southwest were known to sort through animal and human poop looking for certain

prized undigested grains and seeds. These would then be removed, cleaned, roasted, ground, and eaten.

This process of getting food from poop was called the "Second Harvest."

Plenty of other people have eaten poop too, usually out of the belief that it was good for them. For instance, it's reported that Martin Luther (1483–1546) enthusiastically ate a spoonful of his own poop each day. Now *that's* a hearty breakfast!

PROFESSIONAL FACE-STUFFERS

It's not only *what* we eat that can be gross, but also *how* we eat it. For instance, consider the International Federation of Competitive Eating. This group puts on events in which a professional eater like Joey Chestnut can stuff sixty-six hot dogs down his throat in twelve minutes.

If you've ever watched this kind of eating before, you know that it's definitely gross. And since there are already WAY too many people in the world eating way too much food, do we really want to encourage more of the same?

Instead, we should be fans of the group that puts on "air-eating championships."[2] This is a lot like playing air guitar. But instead of pulling out an imaginary guitar, contestants eat imaginary food! Ironically, the winner of the first air-eating competition later turned out to be an air-bulimic! ("I pretended to throw up," he said. "It was a pretend cry for help.")

CANNIBALISM

Think about this: people eat almost all primates, including chimpanzees. (In Africa, chimps fall under the category of something called "bush meat.")

I'm amazed that humans eat primates at all. It seems so wrong. Did you know that chimpanzees have 98 percent of the same genetic code as humans? That means eating a chimp would be 98 percent cannibalism!

I JUST ASKED MY WIFE IF SHE WOULD EAT A CHIMPANZEE. HER REPLY: "IF I WAS IN AFRICA AND I WAS HUNGRY AND IT WAS LEGAL, SURE. I'D EAT A CHIMPANZEE."

2.   The Citizens for Smaller Portions and More Petite Tummies.

THIS WAS A SURPRISE! "BUT WOULD YOU EAT A PERSON?" WAS MY NEXT QUESTION.

"IF IT HAD ENOUGH SEASONING," WAS HER ANSWER.

Apparently, I need to keep lots of groceries in the house.

Cannibals have been around for a very long time in a whole lot of places. There's historical evidence of cannibalism on all of the continents (except Antarctica). There are bones of human ancestors in Spain from 800,000 years ago that show signs of people eating people. And cannibalism may explain what happened to the Neanderthals. This species

DEAD MEN TELL NO TALES ... AND THEY'RE SO TENDER!

"Tender as a dead man" is a phrase still sometimes heard on the South Pacific island of Fiji. (But my travel agent says there haven't been any cannibals there for a long time.)

of human disappeared about 35,000 years ago. (You know, they're the ones with receding foreheads and prominent brow ridges. No, not your gym teacher!)

Recent evidence suggests that modern humans (that's us) ate them! Neanderthal bones have been found bearing the same marks that were left on deer carcasses by our ancestors.

There are some famous stories about cannibalism in the modern age. You probably already know about the eighty-seven pioneers who were stranded at Donner Pass in 1846.

Forty of them got eaten! And of course, there are the astronauts stranded on Mars who ate each other in 2092. But you may not have heard of Alfred Packer. He was a prospector looking for gold in Colorado who was trapped by a blizzard along with some other miners.

Packer survived by eating his colleagues. At his trial, the judge who sentenced Packer to thirty years in jail said, "You are a low-down, depraved son-of-a-[gun]. There were only seven Democrats in Hindale County, and you ate five of them!"

In the twenty-first century, we seem to have left cannibalism behind. But odd echoes remain! For example, an animal-rights organization came up with an idea to sell George Clooney–flavored tofu. The idea was that they would use the sweat from Clooney's gym towel to flavor some bean curd. They even came up with a name for it: CloFu.

NONE WAS EVER MADE, THOUGH. AS FOR GEORGE CLOONEY'S RESPONSE, HE SAID, "AS A MAMMAL, I'M OFFENDED."

But if you think that's bad, then listen to this: a man named Mark Nuckols invented a human-flavored tofu called Hufu. The bean curd's flavor was based on what cannibals described humans as tasting like. The Hufu motto: It's the healthy human-flesh alternative.

Kicking the Bucket

It's a tragedy, but death is a fruit that all of us must take a bite from someday.

Man, I am so poetic! And at one time I would have been brave, too. That's because lots of people used to avoid talking (or even thinking!) much about death. But this all changed when a new force entered our culture. It's a force so powerful, it has been able to sweep aside our old prejudices while allowing us to look at death more closely.

Yes, I'm talking about the *CSI* television shows. (All twenty of them!) The success of *CSI* has made it okay for people of all ages to consider death. (Especially if murder

HANGING AROUND

In 1634, a man named John Bartendale was hanged for more than thirty minutes before being buried. Later that day, a person passing Bartendale's grave saw the earth on it moving. The brave soul dug out the still-living executed man! Bartendale's profession was a "piper," and between his strong neck and big lungs, he'd survived! A judge later ruled that since Bartendale had already been executed, he had paid his penalty and was free to go.

is involved!) And maybe this isn't a bad thing. After all, although it's the biggest cliché of all time, death is part of life. So why not learn more about it? And since death is such a deadly serious topic, my theory is that while learning about it, we have to joke about it. The only other option is crying!

Joking about death is sometimes called "gallows humor" or "black humor." Here's an example: An elderly man was dying at home when he smelled an apple pie baking. He loved apple pie! He managed to get out of bed and stagger into the kitchen, and there it was—*delicious!* The old man was reaching for the pie when his wife yelled, "Keep away! That's for your funeral."

Anyway, *CSI* has taught me a lot. For example, I now know there are special schools that provide in-depth classes for police officers and advisors who investigate death scenes. Just outside of Austin, Texas, is an "outdoor composition research facility." This is a place where dead human bodies are left outdoors in the sun and rain for various lengths of time. Students then study the body's decomposition. This helps them make informed decisions later in their careers!

WHAT'S SO SCARY ABOUT DEAD PEOPLE?

In the Indian city of Ahmadabad is a place called the New Lucky Restaurant. This business was founded in the 1950s in an unusual spot: a cemetery! Inside the restaurant are several gravestones, but the customers don't care. One local professor explained it this way: "Graveyards in India are never scary places. We don't have a literature of horror stories so we don't have much fear of ghosts."

Along with funeral home workers, these future *CSI* officers are "death professionals," and they are trained to notice certain things. For example, they might notice that a dead body has more than one color. That's because blood settles, so whatever the body's position, any part that's elevated will look paler.

The corpse will probably be in a state of rigor mortis by the time the professionals get there. That is, once the person's blood stops circulating, the body's muscles freeze up, making the "stiff" stiff. Rigor mortis starts at the body's head and then works its way down the body. It's sort of weird, though; rigor mortis can "freeze" a person's face into an expression even though the rest of the body is still limber! But after forty-eight hours, rigor mortis wears off entirely.

Stiff or not, a new dead body is usually called "fresh." Let's learn how it gets stale!

WHAT HAPPENS WHEN? A NOT-VERY-FUN FUN PRIMER!

1 Right after a person dies, he or she starts to decay fairly quickly. The first thing that happens is that the body's cells break down. Their own enzymes digest them, which is actually pretty handy. In fact, I know this is supposed to be gross, but it seems so perfectly natural!

As the cells break down, the bacteria that is naturally inside the body helps out the decay process by eating it. The whole body is a smorgasbord, and everything must go! And as those bacteria eat, they make gas—just like when you're alive.

BUT THE PROBLEM WITH A CORPSE IS THAT IT CAN'T USE BELCHES OR FLATULENCE TO GET RID OF THAT GAS. SO THE BODY STARTS TO INFLATE. BLOATED CORPSES USUALLY GET BIG IN THE GUT AREA BECAUSE THAT'S WHERE MOST OF THE BACTERIA ARE.

This gassy, bloated period goes on for about a week.

2 If the body is left out in the open, some bugs and other small creatures will be attracted to it. Flies will lay eggs in any of the body's wet orifices. Flies never just lay one egg when they can lay a hundred instead. The fly larvae are called maggots, and they will start eating the body's decaying flesh. Maggots look like rice kernels that are moving around, and when a bunch of them start eating, they apparently sound like a bowl of Rice Krispies after milk is poured on them. (Seriously.)

★ Just like adult flies, maggots don't have teeth. To eat, they spit up digestive juice on their food. Then they drink the liquefied leftovers.

3 Special flesh-eating beetles also show up to chow down on the body's skin and muscle tissue. Known as dermestid beetles, these bugs are ALL business. If a dead body is on a wool rug, these beetles and their larvae will eat the body down to the bone, and then eat the rug for dessert! While this sounds disgusting, we should be thankful for the job maggots and carnivorous beetles do! It's also nice that they almost always stick to eating dead tissue. (Every once in a while, a fly will sneak up a living person's nose to lay eggs. The affected person won't know what's happening until he feels something moving up there. He might blow his nose and find maggots mixed with the mucus. Then it's time to call a doctor FAST because maggots can eat through a nose pretty quickly.)

4 After it stops bloating, a decaying body can get down to the business of liquefying. Yep, if you leave it to its own devices, most of the human body will dissolve and melt away. It's actually a good system. (You just don't want to be around when it happens!)

Since you'll probably never smell a decaying human, writer Mary Roach researched it for you. She says a dead person smells "sweet but not flower-sweet. Halfway between rotting fruit and rotting meat."

EXTRA CREDIT: Can you guess one good reason why the tradition of bringing aromatic flowers to a funeral began?

By the way, anything near a decomposing body will get soaked with body liquid. That's why *CSI* officers know that the earth around a murder victim is important. How much gushy stuff has absorbed into it? Answering this question helps tell how long the body's been there. It also helps the investigator decide if he should throw his shoes away.

First, the body's guts and lungs start turning to liquid. Luckily, as these internal organs decompose, they do so under the privacy of whatever skin is still hanging on. (Of course, the bacteria inside the body cause the skin over the belly to start turning green two days after death, so don't look too closely.)

5 As for the brain, it's well protected inside the skull. But because it's pretty soft, it will start leaking out the body's ears, nose, and mouth. (People who suffer head injuries, like boxers and middle-school teachers, sometimes have their brains liquefied while still alive. A doctor who performed autopsies on boxers who died in the ring found that their brains were as goopy as toothpaste.)

6 While decomposition goes on, the bones and teeth of a person stay intact. They're going to be around for a good long time. But without the connecting tendons and muscles, nobody's skeleton stays in one piece!

WHAT I'VE DESCRIBED IS WHAT HAPPENS DURING A BODY'S NATURAL DECOMPOSITION. BUT YOU KNOW HUMANS ... THEY LIKE THEIR BIRTHS NATURAL AND THEIR DEATHS UNNATURAL!

Let me give you an example by using cats. In ancient Egypt, dead pharaohs were dried, stuffed, and wrapped up as mummies. But the pharaohs wanted to have company in the afterlife, so they had their servants killed, dried out, stuffed, and mummified as well.

Oh, and they wanted their cats to be with them too. Lots of cats! They didn't have anything against cats. In fact, they liked felines so much that they wanted to have lots of them as pets in the afterlife. Try guessing the number of Egyptian cats that were made into mummies. Millions and millions and millions! So many cat mummies have been found in Egypt, massive piles of

them were ground up in the nineteenth century and turned into fertilizer.

FUNERAL ARRANGEMENTS

On different continents and at different times, death has been viewed ... differently. But in general, the idea has been to honor people who die, and to try to keep their memory alive. In the African Congo, the Banziri tribe was known to honor the dead by placing the body over a fire. Pots were placed under the burning body to catch the melting oils and dripping fat.

The people would then take this mixture and smear it on their faces. In this way, the dead person was literally still part of the tribe. Then the living people would wash the mixture off their faces and save the water. The dead person's relatives would then drink the water.

Is this cannibalism? I guess! Cannibalism was also practiced in the Southeast Asian islands of Java and New Guinea. For these people, being eaten wasn't a form of punishment. It was a show of respect! If an elder member of the tribe were getting close to dying, he would be spared the indignity of a long, drawn-out illness. Instead, someone would stab him with a bamboo knife. His head would be removed.

The rest of the body would be cooked and eaten by the whole tribe. But the head was reserved for the young men, who would eat the elder's brains. Raw.

And on the nearby island of Borneo, families kept the bodies of relatives in giant jars for one year after their death! The top of the jar was sealed pretty well, but the bottom had a bamboo tube that went outside the home. This allowed the liquefied remains of the person to drain away from the house.

THE GOOD NEWS: After a year, the body was moved to a smaller jar and could be stored outside the home.

THE BAD NEWS: The body had to be moved to a smaller jar.

THE TOWERS OF SILENCE

You wash your hands before you eat. And vultures do the same thing! Except vultures don't have hands. And they use poop instead of soap.

As you probably know, vultures eat rotting meat. But to do so, they have to stand on a dead animal's body. Think of the germs! So to keep their feet from getting infected, vultures poop on them before perching on a corpse.

Starting in the 1990s, India's vulture population plummeted. The birds fell victim to a drug fed to cattle. This was a disaster for the people who used India's "Towers of Silence." You see, there's a religion called Zoroastrianism that has been around since 600 BCE. Its followers do not cremate their dead, nor do they bury them in the earth.

Instead, they "bury" their dead in the sky! This is done by carting a dead body up to a high building called a Tower of Silence. Vultures descend on the corpse and eat it.

THE COMFORTS OF HOME

After burial, a body doesn't have to be lonely. In Madagascar, there is a tradition that takes place about every five years. If a living person dreams of a dead family member, it's considered a sign to dig that relative up! In a ritual called *famadihana*, the body is exhumed and carried through town before being reburied. (In this way, the dead person will remain "comfortable" in the grave.)

But once the vultures started disappearing, the Zoroastrians had to save dead bodies and start raising baby vultures! While they waited for the birds to grow up, they set up big mirrors (or "solar reflectors," if you want to be fancy), which would heat up the bodies and make them decompose quickly.

Most Zoroastrians live in the city of Bombay. So, if the vulture repopulation works, people living in high-rises next to Bombay's Towers of Silence can look out their condo windows to see vultures feasting on corpses. Just like the good old days!

★ Tibetans have a similar view of funerals. After a person dies, there are funeral services for three days. Then the body is cut up and placed on a mountaintop, where it awaits the attention of vultures. This process burns no fuel and requires no land.

NORTH AMERICAN BURIALS

Now let's think about a body taken to a funeral home today. One of the first things that usually happens is the body gets embalmed. (This practice is most common in the United States and Canada.) To do this, two cuts are made, one in a major artery and another in a nearby vein. Then a chemical fluid containing formaldehyde, methanol, ethanol, and solvents is pumped into the body through one tube while the blood is drained out the other.

This embalming fluid slows down the decaying process, so while the body WILL still decay, it won't happen as quickly. It's a modern mummy! Because the embalming fluid is dyed red, it gives the look of life back to the dead. But oddly, while embalming fluid gives the dead body the appearance of life, it is very toxic for anything that's actually alive![1]

That's only the start, though. Preparing a dead body for a traditional coffin burial takes a lot of work. For example, a dead person's jaw tends to hang open. You can sew the jaws together with heavy thread. And a person's eyeballs tend to shrink after death. So to give the eyelids their usual "full" look, funeral home workers tuck little cotton balls under them. Nice.

Also, funeral home professionals are in charge of getting all the poop, urine, and undigested food out of the body. This involves sticking a vacuum tube into the body and, uh, oh dear. Anyway, then embalming fluid is pumped into the stomach, intestines, and bladder. It will stay there for a while, but as the body decomposes, the fluid leaks out of the coffin and into the ground.

1. The World Health Organization lists formaldehyde as a cancer-causing substance.

As for coffins, those that were made of wood were once the standard model. It wasn't uncommon back in the day for a tall corpse to get stuffed unceremoniously into a standard-size pine coffin. What's that, the feet won't fit? They will after you break the dead body's ankles and fold the feet in sideways! Today's coffins come in a range of sizes (thank goodness!) and materials, ranging from metal to cardboard. And since even Costco carries caskets (really!), people have a wide range of shopping options.

But burial is only one option! Cremating, or burning, a body is another ancient tradition that's been gaining popularity

FALLING OFF THE HORSE

While we're used to the idea of burying bodies in cemeteries, one Mongol tradition worked this way: After the funeral was held, the person's body was put on horseback. The funeral crowd then followed the horse until the body fell off, and that spot was where the person was buried.

DON'T CHEW ON YOUR PENCIL!

An artist named Nadine Jarvis makes pencils out of the body's ashes left over after cremation. She can get almost 250 pencils out of an average body's cremains. That's almost a lifetime supply of pencils for family and friends!

in modern times. In fact, about a third of Americans and half of all Canadians choose to be cremated.

In India, open-air funeral pyres are still common, but in places like the United States, high-tech ovens do the heavy lifting. First, the cremation oven heats up to as high as 2,400 degrees Fahrenheit. That's darned hot, but it will still take anywhere from ninety minutes to three hours for the body to be incinerated to seven pounds of ashes. People have found a number of ways to store or return these ashes to nature. One company attaches the ashes to a large biodegradable balloon that drifts away on the wind.

But for some people, cremation raises concerns about global warming and air pollution. Consider India, where bodies are traditionally burned with wood. Since India will soon be the world's most populated country, huge forests must be cut down every year just to provide the fuel for the tens of millions of cremations taking place over just a few months' time.

BUT WHAT WE USUALLY THINK OF AS A "TRADITIONAL" BURIAL (WITH STEEL CASKETS, FORMAL CEMETERIES, AND EMBALMING FLUID) ONLY DATES BACK TO THE LATE 1800S. THE OLDEST AND MOST TRADITIONAL BURIAL STYLE IS ACTUALLY THIS:

WHEN SOMEBODY DIES, YOU BURY THEM. THE END.

Today, this is sometimes called a "green" burial. There is no embalming. If a coffin is used, it's made of biodegradable material like wood, recycled newspapers, bamboo, or even woven banana leaves. This type of coffin decomposes in six months to two years. The body can also be wrapped in a shroud made of cotton or some other natural fibers. A green cemetery looks exactly like a park, because there are no roads or manicured lawns! Some green cemeteries also ban headstones or grave markers. No worries, though. At places like California's Forever Fernwood cemetery, the family is given a Google map with the GPS coordinates of their loved one's location!

Boy, if there's one thing I've learned here, it's that death can be a huge hassle for the relatives of the person who passes away. So to be considerate to my loved ones, I've decided to spare them this anguish. "How?" you ask? Simple: I'll just live forever! (Isn't that what happens when you take a Flintstones vitamin every day?)

GIVING LIFE TO YOUR DEATH SCENES

Actors love playing juicy scenes where they can ham it up. (Now *that's* gross: juicy ham!) And one of the juiciest acting jobs of all time is playing a death scene.

Let's say you've landed a part in a local theater production of *Mary Poppins*. Since you know that a good actor always improvises, you've decided to give your character a death scene. That means you have some important decisions to make! For instance, a good actor should be able to answer these three questions:

1 Who is my character? (Answer: Someone who is going to die.)

2 What does my character feel? (Answer: He feels the icy hand of death on his brow. Or maybe on his neck. Look, it doesn't really matter![2])

---

2. Still, it would be weird to feel the icy hand of death on the bottom of your feet.

3 What does my character want? (Answer: He wants to die, I guess. And if it isn't too much trouble, a Fig Newton would be nice.)

Boy, this is going to be the best death scene in the history of *Mary Poppins*! Let's break down exactly how it's going to work:

THE LEAD-UP

Locate yourself onstage so that the audience can't miss you. Nothing is worse than dying off to the side of the stage where nobody will notice.

THE LAST MOMENT OF LIFE

Decide whether to go for a quick ending or a long one. Of course, long, drawn-out deaths are very tempting. That's why actors love playing the part of Hamlet. After being poisoned, Shakespeare's character says, "I am dead, Horatio." Six lines of dialogue later, Hamlet adds, "Horatio, I am dead." Then eighteen lines after that, Hamlet cries out, "O, I die, Horatio!" And still he goes on for another five lines!

Then he dies. (Surprise!)

As your character's life flutters away, consider some of the following moves:

THE SLOW-MOTION WINDMILL: A slow-motion death is always cool. (And who doesn't like windmills?)

"WHY? WHY? WHY?": Cry it out with feeling and wonder. Optional: "Why, why, why bro?"

"I DIE, HORATIO!"

THE DRAMATIC FALL FROM A HIGH PLACE: Almost impossible to perform in slow motion.

THE LAST-SECOND SHRUG: Right before you drop dead, look out at the audience and give them a shrug along with a look that says, "You win some, you lose some!"

THE FIRST MOMENT OF DEATH

In the entire history of acting, there must have been a time when an actor did a really good death scene and then *actually died.* ("Take a curtain call, Timmy! Uh, Timmy?") If you're concerned about this happening, have the director bring in a stunt person for this part of the scene.

AFTERMATH

You'd think life would be easy after passing away. Not so! You have to decide whether to shut your eyes or to leave them open. Leaving them open will give your corpse a creepy look that will surely distract the audience from the living actors onstage. While this may sound good to you, remember that it's hard not to blink, twitch, or laugh when you're lying there with your eyes open.

But whether your eyes or open or shut, you're probably going to have to lie there for a while until someone pulls the curtain. During this time, try not to breathe too obviously. And avoid sitting up and high-fiving cast members to celebrate your skills.

Oh, last thing: with all that you've learned in this book, you might try doing something that would actually happen to a dead body. Don't do it! Audiences have been known to demand ticket refunds when actors decompose onstage.

EPILOGUE

I've traveled the world looking for gross stuff, and it hasn't always been easy. After stepping on sea cucumber puke in the South Pacific and having to flee cannibals in South Carolina, I decided to take a break and do some hiking in the Swiss Alps.

Ah, Switzerland! What a clean, mountainous country. The Swiss people are so clean-cut, it's hard to imagine any of them wiping a runny nose on their sleeve. And as I hiked on perfectly maintained Alpine trails, I came upon an incredible panorama!

No, not the snow-clad mountains. I'm talking about the six naked backpackers who were clad in nothing but hiking boots!

My first instinct was to run screaming, but I decided to play it cool. (Nothing is worse than having nudists think you're uncool.) So, maintaining eye contact, I walked forward.

MALE HIKER: I can see that you are shocked by our appearance.

ME: Me? Shocked? [Nervous laugh.] Well, maybe a little.

FEMALE HIKER: Ah, but look at this beautiful natural setting. Is it not a paradise?

ME: Uh-huh.

OLDER MALE HIKER: And what did Adam and Eve wear in paradise?

ME: Uh, Adidas sweatsuits?

OLDER FEMALE HIKER: No! They wore nothing. They were innocent children of nature, without the need for shame or personal electronic devices. They saw that the human body is nothing to be ashamed of.

REALLY OLD MALE HIKER: That is why the French call being naked "au naturel." In Germany and Switzerland, we call it the "free body culture."

[At this point, I'm thinking, "Look what gravity does to the human body!"]

ME: Do your "free bodies" do other things besides hike?

REALLY OLD FEMALE HIKER: Yes, we sunbathe, and we also take part in sports like canoeing and horseback riding.

[Here I get woozy imagining naked horseback riders. I hope they put a towel down over the saddle! Then a question comes to me.]

ME: Hey, if naked hikers don't wear clothes, what do you keep in your backpacks?

MALE HIKER: Trail mix! Would you like some, Mr. Uptight American?

As I munched on nudist trail mix and the naked hikers walked off, I realized how small-minded I'd been. Maybe they were right! There's nothing wrong with nudity. I'd been brainwashed! So, slowly at first, and then with greater confidence, I removed my clothing. And then I hiked proudly down the trail with my head held high!

That is, until I came upon a group of elderly women out for a jaunt.

"DISGUSTING!" YELLED ONE WOMAN.

"IT'S HORRIBLE!" CRIED ANOTHER.

"Why is that man wearing underwear?" asked another. (Yes, I'd chickened out and left my underwear on.)

"Good afternoon, ladies," I said. "I can see that you are shocked by my appearance. Ah, but look at this beautiful nature. Is it not a paradise?"

"It *was* paradise," pointed out another, "but you really need to do your laundry."

BIBLIOGRAPHY

Abbott, Geoffrey. *The Executioner Always Chops Twice*. New York: St. Martin's, 2002.

Ahuja, Anjana. "A world without disgust. Discuss." *The Times* (U.K.), January 1, 2007.

Anderson, Danielle. "What Grosses You Out?" *People*, August 22, 2005.

Andrade, C., and B. S. Srihari. "A preliminary survey of rhinotillexomania in an adolescent sample." *Journal of Clinical Psychiatry*, June 2001.

Bakalar, Nicholas. "No Hiding Underarm Odor from Women." *New York Times*, April 21, 2009.

"Beijing's Toilets Go Upscale." Travel in China. http://www.china.org.cn/english/TR-e/19450.htm

Block, Melissa. "First-Year Med Students Enter the 'Gross' Lab." *All Things Considered*, National Public Radio, September 17, 2004.

Bourdain, Anthony. *A Cook's Tour*. New York: Bloomsbury, 2001.

Brandow, Michael. *New York's Poop Scoop Law: Dogs, the Dirt, and Due Process*. West Lafayette, IN: Purdue University Press, 2008.

Branzei, Sylvia. *Grossology*. New York: Price Stern Sloan, 2008.

——. *Grossology and You*. New York: Price Stern Sloan, 2008.

Brody, Jane E. "Babies Know: A Little Dirt Is Good for You." *New York Times*, January 27, 2009.

Brown, Patricia Leigh. "Delicacy of the Wild West Lives On for Those So Bold." *New York Times*, March 18, 2009.

Burnet, John. "In Texas, A Living Lab for Studying the Dead." *All Things Considered*, National Public Radio, June 30, 2009.

Burrell, Brian. *Postcards from the Brain Museum*. New York: Random House, 2005.

"Cannibal Europeans ate their children." Agence France-Press, July 1, 2009.

Chambliss, John. "Student Kicked Off Bus for Passed Gas." *The Ledger*, March 18, 2009.

Conover, Adele. "Hunting Slime Molds." *Smithsonian*, March 2001.

Critchley, Simon. *The Book of Dead Philosophers*. New York: Vintage, 2008.

Dary, David. *Frontier Medicine: From the Atlantic to the Pacific, 1492–1941*. New York: Knopf, 2008.

Dawson, Jim. *Who Cut the Cheese?* Berkeley, CA: Ten Speed, 1999.

——. *Blame It on the Dog.* Berkeley, CA: Ten Speed, 2006.

Elfman, Eric. *Almanac of the Gross, Disgusting & Totally Repulsive.* New York: Random House, 1994.

Erdbrink, Thomas. "In Tehran, the Best Part of Waking Up: A Sheep's Head on Your Plate." Washington Post Foreign Service, March 13, 2009.

Flinn, J. "Movable feast proves one man's meat is another's poison." *San Francisco Chronicle*, April 24, 2005.

"The Food Defect Action Levels: Levels of Natural or Unavoidable Defects in Foods That Present No Health Hazards for Humans." Washington, DC: Food and Drug Administration, Center for Food Safety and Applied Nutrition, rev. 1998, 2005.

Foss, Kanina. "News Report." *The Star* (South Africa), March 3, 2009.

"Foul-smelling felon." *Copenhagen Post*, March 26, 2009.

Fountain, Henry. "A Plant That Thrives When Used as a Toilet." *New York Times*, June 15, 2009. http://www.nytimes.com/2009/06/16/science/16obpitcher .html?_r=1&scp=7&sq=borneo&st=cse

Fraenfelder, Mark. *The World's Worst.* San Francisco: Chronicle, 2005.

Gazzaniga, Michael S. *Human: The Science Behind What Makes Us Unique.* New York: HarperCollins, 2008.

George, Rose. *The Big Necessity: The Unmentionable World of Human Waste and Why It Matters.* New York: Metropolitan, 2008.

——. "Yellow Is the New Green." *New York Times*, February 27, 2009.

Glausiusz, Josie. "Oh, Yuck!" *Discover*, December 2002.

Haber, Dr. Gordon. "Growing Wolf Pups." August 9, 2008. Alaska Wolves, http:// www.alaskawolves.org

Halls, Kelly Milner. "Eeewww . . . GROSS!" *Chicago Tribune*, September 24, 1998.

Hawks, Nigel. "Disease made Karl Marx boil with anger." *The Times Online*, October 31, 2007.

Hillman, Ben. *How Weird Is It? A Freaky Book All About Strangeness*. New York: Scholastic, 2009.

Holmes, Bob. "The three domains of disgust." *New Scientist*, July 05, 2008.

Hopkins, Jerry. *Extreme Cuisine: The Weird & Wonderful Foods That People Eat*. Hong Kong: Periplus, 2004.

"Horror Story Printed on Toilet Paper in Japan." Associated Press, May 24, 2009.

"How to Remove a Leech from an Eyeball." News.com.au http://www.news.com.au/story/0,27574,25361409-13762,00.html

Kaufman, Leslie. "Greening the Herds: A New Way to Cap Gas." *New York Times*, June 5, 2009.

King, Florence. "The Misanthrope's Corner." *National Review*, May 20, 2002.

Landau, Elizabeth. "Spit happens: Saliva's mysteries revealed." CNN.com, March 3, 2009.

Lemonick, Michael. "The Ewww Factor." *Time*, June 4, 2007.

Levy, E. J. "The Maggots in Your Mushrooms." *New York Times*, February 13, 2009.

"The List: The Hardest Places in the World to Find a Bathroom." *Foreign Policy*, August 2008. http://www.foreignpolicy.com/story/cms.php?story_id=4414

"Love means never holding your nose." *New Scientist*, June 17, 2006.

Maxmen, Amy. "Where funny faces come from." *Science News*, July 19, 2008.

Manseau, Peter. *Rag and Bone: A Journey Among the World's Holy Dead*. New York: Holt, 2009.

McKie, Robin. "How Neanderthals met a grisly fate: Devoured by humans." *The Guardian*, May 17, 2009. http://www.guardian.co.uk/science/2009/may/17/ neanderthals-cannibalism-anthropological-sciences-journal

Miller, William I. *The Anatomy of Disgust*. Cambridge, MA: Harvard University Press, 1997.

Nance, Kevin. "Cremation Nation." Obit-Mag.com. May 24, 2009. http://www.obit-mag.com/viewmedia.php/prmMID/5352

National Kidney and Urologic Diseases Information Clearinghouse. http://kidney .niddk.nih.gov/index.htm

Nussbaum, Martha. "Danger to Human Dignity: The Revival of Disgust and Shame in the Law." *Chronicle of Higher Education*, August 06, 2004.

Pang, Kevin. "The ultimate in gag gifts." *Chicago Tribune*, December 12, 2007.

BIBLIOGRAPHY

"Paris race track offering free dung to help planet." Agence France-Presse, April 7, 2009.

Quick, Jason. "The . . . ugh, six sweatiest players." *The Oregonian*, November 16, 2008. http://blog.oregonlive.com/behindblazersbeat/2008/11/the_ugh_six_sweatiest_players.html

Roach, Mary. *Stiff: The Curious Lives of Human Cadavers*. New York: Norton, 2003.

Salkeld, Luke. "Hitler had shocking table manners, gorged on cake and suffered flatulence, reveals never-before-seen profile." *Daily Mail*, February 17, 2009.

Sawer, Patrick. "Revealed: The Secrets of Belly Button Fluff." *The Telegraph*, March 1, 2009.

Schneiderman, R. M., "Under the Knife to Prevent More Cuts." *New York Times,* July 11, 2009.

Sierra, Judy. *The Gruesome Guide to World Monsters*. Cambridge, MA: Candlewick, 2005.

Simon, Scott. "It's Paper, Paper Made of Wombat Poo." *Weekend Edition*, National Public Radio, March 7, 2009.

Stallone, Jacqueline. "Rumpology." http://www.jacquelinestallone.com/rumps.html

Steinfeld, Carol. *Liquid Gold: The Lore and Logic of Using Urine to Grow Plants*. Sheffield, VT: Green Frigate, 2004.

"Switzerland Plans to Fine Naked Hikers." *Der Spiegel*, January 29, 2009.

Tait, Malcolm. "The fate of India's vultures." *Ecologist*, January 10, 2004.

"The Towers of Silence." *Time*, April 1974.

Taylor, Matthew. "Footballer given yellow card 'for breaking wind' during penalty shot." *The Guardian*, April 5, 2009.

Trudeau, Michelle. "What Facial Expressions Are Really Saying." *Morning Edition*, National Public Radio, June 19, 2008.

"Tunbridge Wells strikes back." *Economist*, January 17, 2004

Van Sickle, Abby. "They clean grisly scenes." *St. Petersburg Times*, January 1, 2007.

Walker, Ron. "Dumb and Dumber 2.0." *New York Times Magazine*, January 28, 2009.

"World's Smelliest Cheese Named." BBC News, November 26, 2004.

Wright, Karen. "What the Dinosaurs Left Us." *Discover*, June 1, 1996.

Yoda, Hiroko and Matt Alt. *Yokai Attack! The Japanese Monster Survival Guide*. New York: Kodansha International, 2008.

Zimmer, Ben. "Which Words Do You Love and Which Do You Hate?" *Visual Thesaurus*, May 19, 2009. http://www.visualthesaurus.com/cm/wordroutes/1857/